Diesels and Elec

LOCOMOTIVES INTERNATIONAL SPECIAL EDITION No. 2

A Locomotives International Publication

Above: Russian-built class M62 heavy goods locomotive no. 781.312-4 shakes the ground as it storms through the station and goods yard at Martin in Slovakia in March 1997, the two-stroke 12-cylinder diesel engine emitting a thunderous roar.
Photo: Paul Catchpole.

Front Cover: The first of fifteen English Electric Co-Cos supplied for the electrification of the 5'3" gauge E.F. Santos - Jundiai in Brazil. The locomotive had just arrived at Paranapiacaba with a freight train heading down the famous Serra do Mar inclines on 19th October 1978. *Photo: Günter Koch.*

Title Page: An electric veteran in Chile, one of the 5'6" gauge class E-30 Bo-Bos built in 1961 by Ansaldo and Breda arrives from the south of the country at Santiago's Central Station with the 'Tren del Sur' in April 1996. *Photo: Paul Catchpole.*

ISBN 1-900340-17-8
First Edition. Published by Paul Catchpole Ltd., The Haven, Trevilley Lane, St. Teath, Cornwall, PL30 3JS, Great Britain.
www.locomotivesinternational.co.uk
Printed and bound by Image Design & Print, Bodmin, Cornwall, Great Britain.
British Library Cataloguing in Publication Data. A catalogue record for this book is available from the British Library.

Diesels and Electrics Special Edition No. 2
Locomotives International

Contents

Acknowledgements:

The collective authors of this edition are, in alphabetical order: Paul Catchpole, Paul Engelbert, Wolfgang Ewers, Günter Koch, Nicholas Pertwee, Wilf Simms and Gottfried Wild.

In addition to the principal authors of the various chapters some photographers have provided extra illustrations and their names are credited in the captions to their pictures. Any uncredited photos in each chapter are either the principal author's or have been selected from the principal author's collection.

Crocodiles and Flatirons -
Rod-Drive Electric Locomotives in Austria and Switzerland - *by Günter Koch*

Due to their alpine nature both Austria and Switzerland were predestined for the use of electric railways, and indeed they were among the European pioneers in that field. Several projects had already been carried out before the First World War but it was after the war that work started on a large scale. One of the most important questions, the kind of current to be used, had already been resolved by that time. In 1912 a treaty had been made by the railway administrations of three German States, Prussia, Bavaria, and Badenia, which was subsequently joined by Austria, Switzerland, Sweden, and Norway, specifying that future main line electrification was to be done with single-phase a.c. of 15 kilovolts / $16^2/_3$ hertz. The choice was based on the premise of using alternating current because of its easy convertibility, and on previous experience of three-phase a.c. which, although optimal from the point of view of motor performance, required too complicated a system of catenary, while for industrial single-phase a.c. of 50 Hz frequency no usable traction motor existed. This far-sighted treaty was to facilitate future trans-border traffic considerably.

Most of the locomotives which were subsequently developed had one feature in common: the transmission of torque from motor to wheels by rod drive. Traction motors directly mounted and geared to the axles, such as the nose-suspended type used on tramcars, were unsprung which, considering the weight of powerful motors, would cause poor riding qualities. The tendency was therefore to mount one or two large traction motors on the spring-suspended main frame, but then the movement of motor and wheels relative to each other prohibited the use of a direct gear drive. So the engineers looked to the steam locomotive whose rod drive was flexible enough to absorb all kinds of shock caused by movement.

In most cases the motor was not directly rod-connected to the driving wheels, instead a jackshaft mounted in the main frame was inserted in between. Although the detail designs were different we can distinguish two ways of incorporating a jackshaft drive. In most earlier locomotives a large slow-rotating traction motor was connected to the drive by rod and parallel cranks, i.e. the jackshaft rotated at the same speed as the motor. Later one or two smaller, fast-rotating traction motors were geared to it by a reducing gear drive.

The rod drive suffers from a principal fault. One major advantage of the electric motor as compared to piston engines is that its primary motion is rotational. Transmission of torque by direct gearing does not involve any reciprocating parts which need to be balanced, but the rod drive introduces such parts and hence causes the engine's running performance to deteriorate. It is therefore not surprising that efforts to eliminate it were soon successful, resulting in various forms of single-axle (independent) drive by spring-

Above: Austrian jackshaft and rod drive 1-C-1 No. 1073.17 at Attnang-Puchheim on 10th July 1974.

Left: A classic 'Crocodile', ÖBB No. 1189.07 photographed on the same day in Attnang-Puchheim.

suspended motors. In most countries the construction period of rod-drive electric locomotives for main-line use was therefore short, except for Sweden where they were built until about 1970.

In central Europe a major part of what by now could be called "living fossils" had already disappeared at that time, and they rapidly diminished further. On the Deutsche Bundesbahn just a handful had remained in shunting duties, but in Austria and Switzerland a quite surprising variety survived a little longer. What made them so attractive was that they had played a role in the first act of a dramatic technical stage play, and even a strict supporter of steam traction could find examples whose visual appearance frankly testified to their origins. Look at ÖBB locomotive 1073.17

The classic Swiss 'Crocodile', SBB Ce 6/8 no. 14282 at Buchs, 30th July 1975.

portrayed at Attnang-Puchheim (opposite page, upper), and imagine the long hood transformed into a boiler with side tanks, the small rear hood into a coal bunker, the jackshaft into a coupled wheelset, cylinders and some other items added, and art of magic will create a perfect 2-8-2 tank locomotive.

The ÖBB class 1073 was one of three types developed for the electrification of the Arlberg and Salzkammergut lines which the Bundesbahnen Österreich (BBÖ) carried out from 1923 to 1926*. The Arlberg railway leads from the Tyrolean capital, Innsbruck via Landeck and the Arlberg Pass to Bregenz on Lake Constance where it connects with the German and Swiss state railways. It is a typical alpine main line with grades of 2.64% (1 in 38) on the eastern and 3.14% (1 in 32) on the western ascent, at a minimum curve radius of 225 m. Conditions on the Salzkammergut railway from Attnang-Puchheim to Stainach-Irdning, with a ruling grade of 2.5% (1 in 40), are only slightly easier. The engine, originally designated BBÖ class 1029, was designed as a light express locomotive of 1'C1' wheel arrangement and 14.5 t axle load that could haul 210 tons at 36 km/h on a 1 in 40 grade and 170 tons at 34 km/h on a 1 in 32 grade. The two traction motors of 2 x 500 kW one-hour output were mounted on the main frame and geared to a common jackshaft mounted between and in line with the second and third coupled axle, i.e. the connecting rod to the second (driving) wheelset was horizontal and congruent with the coupling rods. Due to weight limitations only a single cab was fitted at the engine's rear end. To provide visibility for the driver the long hood in front of the cab which houses the high-tension equipment, transformer, traction motors, air blowers, etc, had to be kept narrow. The small hood at the front housed the vacuum pumps while that behind the cab enclosed the compressor. Vacuum braking was used on the BBÖ but was later replaced by air braking. Twenty locomotives were built by AEG and StEG/Vienna from 1923 onwards, but only eleven survived World War 2 and were subsequently modernised. Thus the traction motors received new windings, which increased their one-hour ratings to 2 x 580 kW power, 67 kN tractive force, while the speed could be raised from 75 to 80 km/h. The last were retired in 1975.

The second of the Arlberg types was projected as a "heavy mountain express" locomotive, BBÖ class 1100, which was to become ÖBB class 1089/1189 after World War 2. An example of this most impressive design is seen in the shape of ÖBB 1189.07 (opposite page, lower). "Heavy", in this context, meant total weight or tractive force, but not axle load which, as said before, was restricted to 14.5 tons. The projected hauling capacity was 360 tons at 50 km/h on a 1 in 33 and 300 tons at 45 km/h on a 1 in 32 grade. What came out was an articulated or "double" locomotive of type (1'C)'(C1')', copied from a Swiss "Gotthard" type developed three years earlier (and to be discussed next). But taking a closer look, and remembering that a class 1073 electric might, by witchcraft or imagination, be transformed into a 2-8-2T - would this class 1189 with the art of magic not yield a perfect 2-8-0 + 0-8-2 Garratt? I do not know if the Swiss and Austrian engineers of that time had any knowledge of the Garratt at all. The first "experimental" main line Garratt, class GA of the South African Railways, had just been outshopped, and little if any of the results achieved in operation may have leaked through to Europe. But even if the Europeans had not been aware of Garratt's development, the conclusion to be drawn is: a sound idea, when its time comes, may have more than one inventor, and more than one application!

Let's finish with magic art and return to reality and hard facts. The project was entrusted to the Swiss Brown Boveri Co. (BBC) which had developed the Gotthard prototype, with the Wiener Lokomotivfabrik (WLF) responsible for the mechanical part. The two engine trucks were close-coupled to each other for transfer of push-pull forces. Each truck carried two traction motors geared to a common jackshaft, arranged between and connected to the first and second coupled axles. Due to profile limitations the jackshaft centre was 30 mm above driving wheel centres, hence the connecting rods were very slightly inclined. Other components such as air blowers, compressors, vacuum pumps, etc. were also mounted under the low hoods on the bogies, while the central superstructure pivoted to the bogies comprised the driver's cabs at each end, with the transformer and other electric equipment in between.

The first batch of seven locomotives was supplied 1922-24

* Footnote: The state railways of Austria were Bundesbahnen Österreich (BBÖ) from 1919 to 1938 and Österreichische Bundesbahnen (ÖBB) from 1945 onwards. During the "Anschluss" to Germany 1938-1945 they were part of the Deutsche Reichsbahn (DR).

and designated BBÖ class 1100. Their maximum speed was 70 km/h, one-hour ratings were power 1800 kW, tractive force 120 kN. A second batch of nine, designated BBÖ class 1100.100 and built 1926/27, and slightly more powerful motors yielding one-hour ratings of power 1900 kW, tractive force 123 kN, speed 75 km/h. One from the first batch was destroyed in WW2 while the remainder became ÖBB classes 1089 and 1189 respectively. Their nickname "Crocodile" which they had adopted from their Swiss antetype, is self-explanatory. Their last home depot was Attnang-Puchheim from where they mainly worked the Salzkammergut line before the last were retired in 1979, but a few have been preserved.

Switzerland could boast a variety of "crocodiles" but the archetype which gave its name to the whole family was SBB's (1'C)'(C1')' class Ce 6/8 developed for the electrification of the Gotthard railway. Surprisingly, conditions on this line are rather less severe than on the Arlberg. Its ruling grade had been restricted to 2.5% (1 in 40), with 300 m minimum radius, at the expense of making extensive use of spiral tunnels. Electric operation of the summit tunnel started in June 1920, the whole mountain section Erstfeld-Bellinzona was ready in May 1921. It is interesting to note that the prototype supplied by SLM and BBC in 1919, designated Ce 6/8^I No. 14201, was not a "crocodile" by its external appearance, as it had a long main superstructure extending above the six coupled wheelsets, with only short low hoods at the extreme ends. The slim form of a reptile came with the 33 series locomotives of class Ce 6/8^{II} built 1920-22 by the Swiss Locomotive and Machine Factory (SLM, Winterthur), with the Machine Factory Oerlikon (MFO) supplying the electrical equipment, followed in

SBB De 6/6 no. 15303 runs beside the road at Emmen on 20th November 1982.

1926/27 by eighteen similar but more powerful engines of sub-class Ce 6/8^{III}.

The SBB crocodiles were projected as heavy freight locomotives. In comparison with their Austrian successors they were heavier but at the same time shorter, which gave them a distinctly more compact appearance. Surprisingly they were less powerful, with one-hour ratings of 1650 and 1810 kW for the two sub-classes, but due to a higher transmission ratio they developed higher tractive forces of 165 and 186 kN (one-hour) respectively. The general arrangement was similar to that of the Austrian engines just described, but the jackshafts were positioned higher and the connection to the drivers was different. The Ce 6/8^{II} had the drive on the first coupled wheelset of each bogie, with the connecting rod designed as a flat triangle slotted vertically to receive the crank pin of the driving wheel, which could thus slide in its guide. The other end of the triangle was connected to an auxiliary ("blind") crankshaft mounted in front of the drivers. The second and third coupled wheelsets were connected by coupling rods. The arrangement, which efficiently compensated for spring deflections but was quite complicated, is clearly seen on locomotive 14282 (previous page). In contrast the Ce 6/8^{III} had inclined connecting rods to the third coupled axles, with the second and first coupled wheelsets connected by coupling rods, an arrangement that became known as the "Winterthur inclined rod drive".

From 1942 to 1947 thirteen of the Ce 6/8^{II} were rebuilt with more powerful motors, raising the one-hour ratings to 2680 kW power and 214 kN tractive force. With the speed increased to 75 km/h they were re-classed Be 6/8^{II}. The permissible speed of class Ce 6/8 III was subsequently also raised to 75 km/h, without modifications, and the class re-classified accordingly Be 6/8^{III}. Some of the remaining Ce 6/8^{II} were rebuilt for shunting duties and in this form

SBB 'Flatiron' E 3/3 no. 16355 at Sargans on 3rd April 1974

ÖBB 'Flatiron' no. 1161.017 at Bischofshofen on 1st September 1987.

ratings of 430 kW power / 56.4 kN tractive force and a permissible speed of 40 km/h. They were built in large numbers from 1928 to 1966 with only minor modifications, e.g. a more powerful motor was later used yielding one-hour ratings of 500 kW power / 61.4 to 68.7 kN tractive force. The example shown in the photo (opposite page, lower), No. 16355, was built in 1932 to the original specifications. Many of them are still in regular service today.

Austria also had its flatirons, but these had four coupled axles in order to compensate for the low permissible axle load of 14 tons at the time they were designed. A single motor of 720 kW one-hour output was placed on top of the jackshaft, mounted between the first and second axle, with a Winterthur inclined rod drive acting on the third axle. The one-hour tractive force was 80 kN, the permissible speed 40 km/h. Five locomotives designated BBÖ class 1070 were built by AEG-Union and WLF in 1926, and sixteen more powerful locos rated at 750 kW power / 86 kN tractive force followed 1928-32 as BBÖ class 1070.100. Under DR management they became class E61 and six more were built 1941/42. The post-war ÖBB renumbered them class 1061/1161. The example shown above, 1161.017, is the first of the DR-built wartime locomotives. Finally, twelve similar but much heavier locomotives of 17 t axle load designated class 1062 were built in 1955.

Let us stay with Austria, as the third of the Arlberg types still needs to be discussed. This was projected as a freight locomotive able to haul 340 or 290 t at 30 km/h on the 1 in 38 or 1 in

outlived their companions. One of the last in regular service was 14282, photographed on a foggy 30th July 1975 on the hump at Buchs, S.G. (page 5).

The SBB had yet another such reptile, nicknamed the "Seetal crocodile" as it had specifically been developed for the Seetal (Lake Valley) Railway, Wildegg - Emmenbrücke. This rural branch, built 1883 by an originally British company, links with the Zürich-Aarau and Olten-Luzern main lines at Lenzburg and Emmenbrücke respectively. It has grades of up to 3.8% (1 in 27) and runs tramway-style through the main streets of some of the towns along its way, as shown by De 6/6 15303 at Emmen on the opposite page (upper).

As early as 1910 it was electrified with 5.5 kV / 25 Hz a.c., but in 1922 was taken over by the SBB and in 1930 converted to 15 kV / 16⅔ Hz. When the three C'C' locomotives of class De 6/6 were put into service 1926 they were consequently designed for dual current operation. Each bogie had one single motor of 430 kW one-hour output and the Winterthur inclined rod drive just described. The one-hour tractive force was 56.4 kN per bogie, the permissible speed of 40 km/h was later raised to 50 km/h.

So that's quite a few crocodiles already, but what about flatirons? The recipe is simple: take a De 6/6 crocodile, cut it through in the middle, and there is a pair of Ee 3/3 "flatirons". Indeed this was the recipe followed by the SBB when the rapid growth of electrification required suitable shunting power. Some early examples even had their cab at one end, as would result from the procedure described, but later the cab was placed in the centre.

The Ee 3/3 was a semi-De 6/6 in any respect, except for the electric equipment which was of course single-current. The motor, the Winterthur inclined rod drive, even the wheel diameter and bogie wheelbase were identical, as were one-hour

Austrian rod-drive electric no. 1080.01 at Eisenerz in the company of iron ore hopper wagons on 12th June 1974.

32 grades of the Arlberg east and west ramps respectively. The project was carried out by Siemens & Halske of Austria with Krauss, Linz, for the mechanical part, and resulted in a ten-coupled outside-framed locomotive of quite unusual design. Its five axles were coupled together by rods mounted on Hall cranks, but only the three central axles were powered by nose-suspended motors of 340 kW each, while the two unmotorised outer axles, mounted with side play, were driven by coupling rods, certainly not a "rod drive" in its strict sense. The locomotive had end-cabs, with short low hoods in front housing the compressor and vacuum pumps. One-hour ratings were power 1020 kW, tractive force 113 kN, and the maximum speed was 50 km/h. Twenty locomotives designated BBÖ class 1080 were supplied 1924/25 which became class E88 during the DR period, but regained their original designation 1080 on the post-war ÖBB. The first of its class, 1080.01, is shown on the previous page at Eisenerz, base of the famous Erzberg rack line which was then still in full swing.

Ten locomotives of an improved version designated BBÖ class 1080.100, later ÖBB class 1180, were supplied 1926/7. They were heavier, as the permissible axle load had been raised to 16 tons, and more powerful with one-hour ratings of 1300 kW power / 130 kN tractive force, and were equipped with electric resistance brakes. Externally they differed as the small front hoods had been omitted and the cabs drawn forward to the front ends. As an example 1180.05 is seen above.

The small 1'B1' numbered ÖBB 1072.05, photographed as

the last of her class at Wien Praterstern (above), does not give the impression of great importance, but the railway for which it was built was one of the pioneers in Austrian electrification. The "Localbahn Wien-Pressburg", opened by a private company in 1914, connected Vienna with Bratislava, then a provincial capital of the Austro-Hungarian Monarchy, and was electrified from its beginning. The end sections leading right into the city centres had the 600 V d.c. "tramway" system while the 51 km long interurban section used 15 kV / $16^2/_3$ Hz a.c., locomotives being exchanged at change-of-system stations. The locomotive shown, of which eight were built from 1913 to 1916, was developed by AEG-Union in co-operation with Graz Wagon Works. A slow-rotating motor of 600 kW output was mounted on the main frame and connected via parallel cranks and connecting rods inclined by 45° to the jackshaft, mounted in line with the drivers. The latter were connected by coupling rods secured in eyes on the connecting

Heading a goods train at Leissigen on 20th August 1979 is BLS Ce 4/4 no. 308, an example of the series modernised from a Ce 4/6 1-B-B-1 wheel arrangement.

Below: A Te 2/3 is half a Ce 4/6! BLS Te 2/3 no. 32 is illustrated at the summit station of Kandersteg on 24th August 1979.

a minimum curve radius of 220 m. The existing Spiez-Frutigen section of 13.5 km length was electrified in 1910 with a.c. at 15 kV / 15 Hz, soon modified to 15 kV / $16^2/_3$ Hz, and served as a test bed for various prototype locomotives. The mountain section opened to traffic in 1913.

Experience gained from the prototypes resulted in a heavy 1'E1' electric, class Be 5/7, of which thirteen were supplied by SLM/MFO in 1913. These impressive engines of 1840 kW one-hour output and 75 km/h speed were the largest pre-World War I electrics in Europe, but were retired in the 1940s and only one has survived in the Verkehrshaus der Schweiz (Traffic House of Switzerland) museum at Luzern. When the other, less graded lines of the BLS Group were electrified in close sequence from 1920 onwards a series of seventeen light (1'B)'(B1')' locomotives designated Ce 4/6 were ordered, again from SLM/MFO. Each bogie had one motor of 368 kW one-hour output, geared to a jackshaft mounted between the driving axles slightly above wheel centres. The connecting rod was vertically slotted so that the jackshaft crankpin could slide in it. Ten were reconstructed 1954-56 as B'B' locomotives of class Ce 4/4, by removing the carrying axles and short hoods in front of the cabs and cutting the bogie frames back. They worked local freight and survived their non-rebuilt analogues by several years. Ce 4/4 No. 308 is shown at the top of the page on 20th August 1979.

Another derivative of the Ce 4/6 is Te 2/3 No. 32 pictured a few days later (above). In 1925 the BLS had received two railcars composed of a half Ce 4/6 locomotive close-coupled to a coach supported on a single front axle and a rear four-wheel bogie. Quite aptly they were nicknamed "Halbesel" (semi-donkey), and they retained that name when in 1956 the appendages were removed and the vehicles rebuilt into 1'B "tractors" for use on

rod. When the BBÖ assumed control in 1921 the engines were designated class 1005. Two were lost during WW2, with the remaining six subsequently becoming ÖBB class 1072. A modernisation program in which the bodies were renovated with rounded edges, changed their appearance considerably. 1072.05 was retired in 1975 but 1072.01 has survived as a working museum-piece.

The Swiss Bern-Lötschberg-Simplon Railway (BLS) was another pioneer in a.c. electrification. In 1906 the Canton of Bern had decided to build the link from Frutigen across the Lötschberg Pass to Brig in the Rhone valley, and had formed a company called Berner Alpenbahn-Gesellschaft to construct and operate it. The company took over the already existing cantonal lines, especially the approach route Thun-Spiez-Frutigen, and decided that the railway should operate with electric traction. From Frutigen (elevation 783 m) the line ascends within 26.5 km to an elevation of 1244 m in the summit tunnel and then descends within a further 34 km to 681 m at Brig, with a ruling grade of 2.7% (1 in 37) and

permanent way duties.

The metre gauge Rhätische Bahn could boast of four different electric systems, by reason of its complicated history. The RhB trunk system had been built from 1889 to 1912 and comprised the Davos line Chur-Landquart-Davos-Filisur, the Albula line Chur-Reichenau-Filisur-Samedan-St. Moritz, with a branch to Pontresina, and the Rhine Valley line Reichenau-Disentis. It had grades up to 4.5% (1 in 22) and curve radii down to 100 m on the Davos line, and was steam-operated throughout.

Electrification with 11 kV / 16²/₃ Hz a.c. started 1913 when the Engadine line Samedan-Scuol was built, with the connecting Samedan-St. Moritz and Pontresina sections electrified at the same time. The rest of the system followed between 1919 and 1922. Then in 1942/3 three independent railways were merged

into the RhB: firstly, the Bernina Railway from St. Moritz via Pontresina to Tirano in Italy, opened 1907 with grades up to 7% (1 in 14.2), curve radii down to 45 m, and electrified at 1000 V d.c., secondly the Chur-Arosa Railway opened 1914, with grades of 6% (1 in 16.7), curve radii of 60 m, and electrified at 2200 V d.c., and finally the isolated Bellinzona-Mesocco line opened 1907, also with 6% grades but electrified at 1500 V d.c., which no longer exists.

When the Engadine line with its relatively gentle grades of 2.5% (1 in 40) began to operate in 1913 it was decided that small 1'B1' locomotives of class Ge 2/4 should suffice for light passenger trains, and seven units numbered 201-7 were ordered from SLM/BBC. A slow-rotating motor of 210 kW output connected by rod and parallel cranks to a jackshaft arranged between and in line with the drivers. Five locomotives were later fundamentally rebuilt in the RhB Landquart Works, with a complete change of the electric equipment, and one of these, No. 221 ex-203, is seen at the top of the page. Its reconstruction in 1945 had involved the installation of a fast-rotating motor of 428 kW output which was geared to the existing jackshaft by gear drive, raising the tractive force from 26.1 to 39.2 kN. Despite its different appearance, the RhB "flatiron" Ge 2/4 No. 212, (above), had similar origins as it was reconstructed from No. 206 for shunting purposes. In this case a fast-rotating motor of 219 kW one-hour output was fitted, and was geared to the existing jack-shaft by a double-gear drive of 1:8.42 gear ratio. The locomotive body was also completely remodelled with a central cab and low hoods.

Veteran RhB Ge4/6 no. 353, seen at Samedan on 21st July 1984, is now reserved for hauling special services.

Rhaetian Bahn Ge 6/6 'Crocodile' no. 413 runs through magnificent scenery near Celerina on 21st July 1984.

For heavier trains, eight 1'D1' locomotives of class Ge 4/6 were received from SLM between 1912 and 1918, with the electrical equipment provided by BBC (two locos), MFO (five locos), and AEG (one loco). They had two slow-rotating motors, of different design depending on their suppliers, rated at 210 kW in the earlier and 280 kW in the later examples. A triangular rod frame on parallel cranks connected the motors to a jackshaft which was arranged in the locomotive centre in line with the drivers. The one-hour tractive force was 52 or 67 kN respectively. One locomotive, No. 353, built in 1914 by SLM/MFO, has survived in working order (above) and is occasionally used for special duties such as hauling a "centenary" train that includes open observation cars.

The electrification of the other RhB trunk lines, carried out in close succession from 1919 to 1922, required new and more powerful locomotives. The result was the "Rhaetian Crocodile" class Ge 6/6, in my opinion one of the best of its kind ever produced, both with respect to efficiency and aesthetics. Fifteen of these C'C' electrics were built between 1921 and 1929 by SLM, with BBC and MFO supplying the electrical equipment. Each of the two bogies carries one motor of 396 kW one-hour output, geared to the jackshaft positioned between the first and second axle, with a Winterthur inclined rod driving on the third axle. The locomotive yields a one-hour tractive force of 95 kN, its permitted speed is 55 km/h. No. 413, illustrated above, was built in 1929. They remained in regular service well into the 1990s and a few were preserved in working order for hauling "nostalgy" trains.

We return to Austria for a last encounter. The ÖBB has one electrified narrow gauge line of 760 mm gauge, called the Mariazeller Bahn as it leads from St. Pölten, 60 km West of Vienna, to Austria's most important place of pilgrimage, Mariazell in the Styrian Alps, and onwards to Gusswerk. The line of 92 km length, with grades of 2.7% (1 in 37), was opened in 1907 with steam traction. The locomotives of class Mh, 0-8-0s with four-wheel support tender which were specially developed for this railway, are better known to steam enthusiasts as ÖBB class 399 of Gmünd narrow gauge fame (where they still haul tourist excursions on summer weekends). On their original line however, in spite of being able to haul 120 ton trains they were hopelessly overworked, as the volume of traffic, both passenger and freight, was already excessive in the first year of operation. In consequence it was decided to electrify the line with a.c. of

ÖBB 1099.09 of the 760mm gauge Mariazeller Bahn photographed at Obergrafendorf on 10th August 1975.

6.5 kV / 25 Hz. Work started without delay and was complete by October 1911.

Sixteen electric C'C' locomotives were supplied by Siemens-Schuckert of Austria and Krauss, Linz. The bogies had outside frames and carried one motor of 210 kW one-hour output, geared to a jackshaft mounted beneath it between the second and third (driving) axles. The rod connecting to them was centrally slotted and acted on Hall cranks, as did the coupling rod to the front axle. With its one-hour tractive force of 46 kN the engine could haul 140-ton trains, but at a much higher speed than the Mh steam locomotives, cutting the travelling time for the full distance by more than one hour. When the BBÖ took over in 1919 they became class E, on the DR they were class E99, and the post-war ÖBB designated them 1099. In the late 1950s a general repair and modernisation scheme was carried out, which permitted the speed to be raised from 40 to 50 km/h. New rounded bodies, similar to the standard gauge engines then being built, were fitted on this occasion and altered their appearance considerably (above). Today they still work the line for which they were built, as the oldest electric locomotives in regular service worldwide.

Literature:

R. Rotter, H. Petrovitsch, Triebfahrzeuge Österreichischer Eisenbahnen, Elektrische Lokomotiven und Triebwagen, Alba, Dusseldorf 1990.
P. Willen, Lokomotiven der Schweiz, 2 volumes, Orell Füssli, Zürich 1972.

TARIF 1: Essential dimensions of locomotives described - Austria / ÖBB. (From: Rotter / Petrovitsch, Ref. 1).

ÖBB class	1161	1072	1073	1080	1180	1189	1099
Gauge, mm	1435	1435	1435	1435	1435	1435	760
Current: Tension, V	15000	15000	15000	15000	15000	15000	6500
Current: Frequency, Hz	$16^2/_3$	$16^2/_3$	$16^2/_3$	$16^2/_3$	$16^2/_3$	$16^2/_3$	25
Wheel arrangement	D	1'B1'	1'C1'	E	E	(1'C)'(C1')'	C'C'
Coupled wheel diameter, mm	1140	1034	1740	1350	1350	1350	800
Carrying wheel diameter, mm	–	870	1034	–	–	870	–
Total wheelbase, mm	5000	5900	9890	7750	7750	17700	7900
Length over buffers, mm	10500	10526	12810	12850	12750	22400	10900
Mass in working order, t	56	56	74	77	81	116	50
Adhesive mass, t	56	28	45	77	81	91.2	50
Number of motors	1	1	2	3	3	4	2
Gear ratio	1:4.69	1	1:4.04	1:6.12	1:6.12	1:3.13	1:3.448
Power (one-hour), kW	750	600	1160	1020	1300	1900	420
Tractive force (one-hour), kN	86	54.5	67	113	130	123	46
Maximum speed, km/h	40	60	80	50	50	75	50

Railways in Slovakia's Tatra Mountains *by Paul Catchpole*

The High Tatras are an area of raw nature on the northern arc of the Carpathian Mountains, straddling the border area of Poland and Slovakia. Today they form one of the Slovak National Parks and are a popular attraction for hikers, skiers and climbers. This region of exceptional natural beauty is the most important area in Slovakia's tourist industry and so is well served by railways and funiculars of various character. A heavily used main line passes along the southern edge of the High Tatras, passing through the principal town of Poprad, from where a network of branch lines serve the area on two gauges, standard (1435mm) and metre.

At the time when railways were first being developed, Slovakia was in the Hungarian half of the Austro-Hungarian dual monarchy so the influences on motive power and railway construction came from Budapest. After the collapse of the Habsburg Empire at the end of the First World War, Slovakia formed the eastern part of Czechoslovakia and so the influence shifted to Prague and the railways came under the authority of the ČSD (Czechoslovakian State Railways). The federal republic of Czechoslovakia was dissolved on 1st January 1993 when Slovakia became fully independent and the railways were re-organised as the Železnice Slovenské Republiky (ŽSR). Today a degree of privatisation has been introduced and the railway system has been renamed the

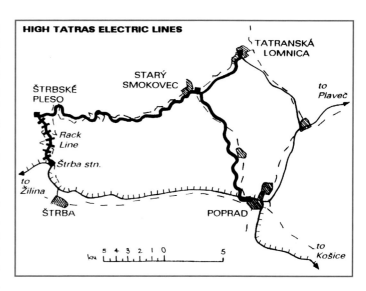

Map from 'Steam and Rail in Slovakia', drawn by Jim Horsford

Železničná Spoločnost (Railway Company).

Tourism in the Tatras started to grow in the late 1880s, following the opening on 18th December 1871 of the Košice - Bohumín Railway (KBD) between Žilina and Poprad-Tatry. The first branch line to be built off this route was the standard gauge Poprad Valley Railway, which was built from Poprad to Spišská Sobota along the valley of the river Poprad. Services were inaugurated on 18th December 1889 and were operated by the KBD. Another branch was built off this line from Studený Potok to Tatranská Lomnica, enabling visitors, especially skiers, to reach the heart of the mountains by rail. From Poprad, at 670 metres above sea level, the line climbs with steep grades and tight curves to reach the branch terminus at 850 metres. The first train ran on 1st September 1895 consisting of a locomotive and one goods wagon.

Motive power on the Poprad Valley Railway was initially a pair of 0-4-0 well tanks obtained second-hand from the Prešov - Tarnów Railway, followed later by four Hungarian-built 0-6-0T, outside-framed versions of the MÁV class 377 subsequently numbered 310.501-504 by the ČSD. The inclines on the branch to Tatranská Lomnica proved too much for these little locos and the KBD obtained six 0-8-0T of MÁV class 475, outside-framed locos with Klein-Lindner axles. These later became ČSD nos. 410.001-006. More recently, trains have consisted of class 850 bogie railcars and class 810 four-wheel railcars, former ČSD classes M286.0 and M152.0 respectively.

Štrba - Štrbské Pleso

The next branch line to be built (opened on 28th July 1896) was a metre gauge rack railway to enable tourists to reach the hotels and lake at Štrbské Pleso. Leaving the main line at Štrba (896m above sea level) it climbed to a terminus at 1350 metres and was operated by a pair of Floridsdorf-built 0-4-0T rack locos built in 1896 and similar to the Austrian Achenseebahn locos. The two Slovak locos became ČSD nos. U29.001/002. The line closed on 14th August 1932 but was re-laid in 1969 in preparation for the 1970 World Ski Championships held in the Tatras.

Rack EMU 405.952-3 prepares for departure from Štrbské Pleso for the descent to Štrba, August 1998. Photo: Author.

An EMU48.0 picks its way between buildings near the Tatra Electric Railway's original terminus at Štrbské Pleso on 25th August 1933.

Photo: Coll. Martin Entner.

The new railway was again metre gauge but was Swiss-built and electrified at 1500 V DC. Most of the route was re-laid on the original alignment, the exception being at Štrbské Pleso where instead of running to the lakeside it now forms an end-on connection to the Tatra Electric Railway (TEŽ) at an interchange built for the World Ski Championships. The trains on the rack railway consist of three twin-unit EMUs built by the Swiss Locomotive Works in 1969. Originally the motor units were numbered EMU29.001-003 and the trailer cars R29.001-003, renumbered around 1989 to 405.951-953 and 905.951-953 respectively.

The Tatranská Elekrická Železnice (Tatra Electric Railway)

The increase in visitors to the Tatras resulting from the opening of the main line was sufficient to warrant the introduction of trolleybuses on a route between Poprad and Starý Smokovec (Old Smokovec) on 2nd August 1904. This service was operated by a couple of local entrepreneurs, Kreiger and Matejka. Unfortunately the operation foundered in 1905, however, the need for public transport did not disappear with the trolleybuses and in the following year the Minister of Transport authorised construction of a metre gauge electric railway.

The 12.8 km 'Vicinal' line constructed between Poprad and Starý Smokovec was opened on 17th December 1908 under its Hungarian company name, the Tatrafuredi Helyiérdeku Villamos Vasutak. From 1922-48 it was known as the Tatranská Elektrická Vicinalná Dráha (TEVD), subsequently becoming the Tatranská Elektrická Železnice, as it remains. The TEŽ continued to be independently operated until 1952 when taken over by the ČSD. As with the rack line, it is electrified at 1500V DC.

Over the years a few changes have been made to arrangements at Poprad. The line used to depart from outside what is now the entrance to Poprad main line station and go eastwards past a small depot before crossing under the standard gauge. Later it was altered to depart in a westerly direction and cross over the main line on a bridge, taking it close to where a new combined metre and standard gauge depot was built in 1968. Poprad station was rebuilt in 1977 and the metre gauge was brought into a terminus above the main line within the same building. The lines on the entrance side of the station were completely removed and a connecting spur to the depot built north of the station.

The first passenger cars were built

EMU48.001 at Poprad during Communist days. (Author's collection).

for the opening of the line by Ganz of Budapest, who supplied some more vehicles in 1912. These latter were three 4-wheel cars, CSD nos. EMU25.001 (used initially for postal services then as a service vehicle), EMU26.001 and EMU28.001, both for passenger service. Three bogie passenger cars were also built by Ganz, EMU48.001-003.

In 1931 the Tatra factory at Smíchov in Prague supplied a bogie vehicle, EMU49.001, which was followed much later, in 1954-56, by five cars, EMU49.002-006, mechanically similar but of completely different appearance. In 1964 the same factory, by then known as ČKD-Tatra, built the first of eighteen three-unit, eight-axle articulated trains. The other seventeen were constructed in 1967-70. Original numbers were EMU89.001-018, later changed to 420.951-968.

In addition to passenger cars, some

An EMU49.0 railcar and Balm/u trailer at Starý Smokovec. Their construction and styling date from the 1950s, as do the fashions of the bystanders. Photo: Jan Koutný.

The first of the pair of Soviet-built TU7E diesels shows both the original and new numbers on its cabside as it shunts stock around Poprad depot yard in August 1998. In the picture below the preserved Ganz four-wheel car EMU26.001 can be seen behind the rather more work-stained diesel.
Photos: Paul Catchpole.

metre gauge locomotives are based at Poprad for use on maintenance trains and around the depot. Nymburk Works converted three of the class T211.0 shunters to metre gauge, creating the class TU29.0, the first of which was allocated to Poprad and the other two to the Čermel Pioneer Railway near Košice. They were renumbered later as 701.951-953. Two other locomotives of standard Russian type TU7E were built in the USSR in 1985 as ČSD TU46.001/002, latterly 706.951/952. As well as performing shunting and works train duties they can also carry snowploughs. The depot at Poprad also has a few special vehicles such as snow-clearers and MUVs (Motorový Universalný Vůz - motorised maintenace vehicles).

The first of fourteen new three-section EMUs of class 425.95 was introduced in September 2000. The design is based on the Stadler GTW 2/6 and features a short central drive unit flanked by a pair of passenger cars. These each include the driver's cab, seating on two levels, ski storage racks and extra capacity for standing passengers. Production was organised as a joint operation between a consortium of companies made up of Stadler, Bombardier and ŽOS Vrútky, with assembly undertaken at Vrútky using components supplied by Stadler and Bombardier. The whole class was operational by July 2002, at which point the

last of the class 420.95 units was withdrawn.

Some standard gauge diesel units, also based on the Stadler GTW 2/6, have been built for the Železničná Spoločnost. Although originally intended for use on the route from Poprad through Studený Potok to Tatranská Lomnica, the first six units went into service in 2003 between Zvolen and Žilina. In their place some class 812 railbuses, modernised, re-motored and upgraded from the class 810, have been allocated instead.

The Hrebeniok Funicular Railway

Some cable-hauled systems in the Tatras come under the authority of the Železničná Spoločnost. Three of these carry aerial cabins but the fourth is a metre gauge funicular railway running about 2km from Starý Smokovec to Hrebeniok. The railway was already in existence before the 1970 World Ski Championships took place but was rebuilt in that year by an Italian company, Ceretti-Tanfani. Near the top of the funicular at Hrebeniok is a large hotel and the starting point for some ski runs, so the line is quite heavily used both in winter and summer.

Above: 405-951-5, a rack railway EMU built in Switzerland by SLM, eases down the gradient into the lower terminus behind the main line station at Štrba.

Above right: The traditional style station building at Starý Smokovec now sees 3-car units built at Vrútky, such as this example seen departing towards Štrbské Pleso.

Above: One of the mid-1950s bogie railcars of series EMU49.0, or perhaps one of the Balm/u tailers. It has survived by virtue of being used by railway staff. The vehicle's purpose is unknown but without pantographs it might perhaps serve as a mobile parts store or workshop.

A young lad on a winter break with his dad watches as the Hrebeniok funicular car creeps the last few metres towards the lower station for the 'lanovka'.

Photos on this page: Paul Catchpole, all taken in January 2004.

Above left: When Slovakia celebrated 150 years of railways in August 1998 the maintenance vehicles were all polished up and displayed outside the shed at Poprad. At the head of the line is a rotary snowplough and beside it one of the class 420.9 three-car units.

Above right: 702-951-5, a standard gauge diesel shunter built at Martin for the ČSD but later converted to metre gauge in order to handle maintenance trains and shed pilot work at Poprad.

Left: A maintenance utility vehicle kept at Starý Smokovec.

Right: The 'new' interchange at Štrbské Pleso, constructed for the 1970 World Ski Championships and occupied by two of the EMU89.0s built at the ČKD-Tatra factory in Smíchov (Prague) to cope with the traffic generated by the event.

Lorries on Rails, Inspection Cars and Draisines on East European Forestry Railways *by Wolfgang Ewers*

Introduction

The era of forestry railways in Eastern Europe is slowly passing into history. The vast Carpathian mountain range - covering an area of approximately 210,000 km$_2$ - once had over 10,000 km of forestry lines with gauges varying between 600 and 760 mm. But in 2004 only one or two lines in Romania (Vişeu de Sus and Covasna - Comandău) and a single forestry railway in Ukraine (Vygoda) survive. Thousands of kilometres of narrow gauge lines in these countries have only recently been abandoned as a result of economic decline and overwhelming road competition - and also as a result of the heavy floods which affected the Carpathian Mountains in 1998. In the following years attempts to reopen the devastated lines proved useless when further floods hit these countries.

In Hungary, however, several lines (the Lenti, the Csömödér, the Kaszó and the Gemenc Forestry Railways) still carry timber but earn their keep by running tourist trains. Many more forestry lines in that country had given up the transport of timber and other freight traffic many years ago in favour of the flourishing passenger

Myndunok Solotvynskyj (or Solotvyno?) at Kilometre 21 on the Vygoda Forestry Railway. During the week some of the line's draisines can almost certainly be found here, such as this speeder and 'GMD-2' lorry. (28.08.2003).

traffic. In Slovakia and Poland three ex-forestry lines have also survived as passenger carrying railways. The Bieszczadzka Kolejka Lesna (Forestry Railway in the Bieszczady Mountains) can be found at Cisna in South Eastern Poland where Poland, Ukraine and Slovakia meet. The Čiernohronská Lesná Železnica (Black Hron Forestry Railway) at Čierny Balog and the Historická lesná úvraťová Železnica (Historic Forestry Reversing Railway) at the Muzeum Kysuckej dediny, Vychylovka meanwhile are situated in central Slovakia near Žilina and Poprad. Forestry locomotives and rolling stock have also joined the assets of closed public, industrial and peat lines at one of the largest preserved European narrow gauge collections at Lavassaare in Estonia.

With steam and diesel locomotives hauling timber trains consisting of bogie flat cars or trucks out of the forests other pieces of rolling stock are often ignored. On the forestry railways of Romania and Ukraine especially, lorries on rails, inspection cars and draisines - light auxiliary rail motor vehicles or trolleys - have played an important operational role. Depending on the type of vehicle they fulfil a variety of tasks. While the inspection cars usually serve the purposes of the track inspectors and the occasional transport of VIPs, the larger draisines are often used by track gangs and foresters. If there is no loco-hauled train available, for example during the night and at weekends, draisines are employed. More or less officially they also carry berry and mushroom pickers into the forests. Last but not least lorries on rails

supply the remote camps of the forest workers and carry equipment. When tracks are in bad condition or have been washed out (something rather common on forestry lines) these lorries are often the only means of transport as they are much lighter than steam or diesel locomotives and are able to run over rough track. On Romanian and Ukrainian forestry railways these vehicles usually outnumber the locomotives. In Hungary and Poland their use has decreased as the lines in these countries are usually much shorter and can be reached by small roads in most cases.

Speeders, AROs and Škodas: The inspection cars

The inspection cars fall in two broad categories: Those cars that have been purpose-built and those that have been converted from road vehicles.

Some of the purpose-built inspection cars are more or less descendants of the speeders, which have been in use since WWI and which were also known as section cars. Their inventor, George Sheffield, created a vehicle that carried officers and men alike for repair crews, messenger services, and whenever it was necessary to get from A to B quickly over the 60 cm gauge railways behind the trenches. A four-wheeled chassis of light construction equipped with a two-cylinder petrol engine and a gear-box are still state-of-the-art some 90 years later. They were built in vast numbers for the narrow-gauge railways in the Soviet Union and

Railway workers returning from their inspection trip over part of the state-owned Borzava Valley line in Ukraine cautiously push their speeder over a level crossing in Irshava. In 2003 passenger services ran over the Vinogradov to Irshava section only. The Priborzhavskoye to Kusnice section is owned by forestry board (27.08.2003).

Below: At Myndunok Solotvynskyj on the Vygoda Forestry Railway, a line to some remote loading locations branches off in the vicinity of a small settlement consisting of just a forester's house and some buildings used by the track gangs. Note the weather protection on the line's track gang speeder, which is badly needed in the rainy summer months. (28.08.2003).

also recall the very similar petrol-engined platelayer's trolleys produced by D. Wickham & Co Ltd. of Ware, Hertfordshire.

A cross between a purpose-built railcar and a converted car is in use on the Hungarian Felsőtárkány Forestry Railway. Numbered 'S04-001', its two-cylinder two-stroke engine and parts of the transmission were taken from the East German 'Trabant' car. When the author visited this line in August 2003 the friendly manager of that tourist-carrying forestry railway happily demonstrated both its rocket-like acceleration and the way that two men can easily jack up the car and turn it using a built-in table. However, the somewhat cramped and poorly sprung four-passenger body offered a fairly bumpy ride!

Further up the comfort range would be an 'ARO' or a 'Škoda': 'ARO' being the Romanian counter-part of the British 'Land Rover' - while 'Škoda' cars, produced at Mladá Boleslav in today's Czech Republic, were built for use only on tarmac roads.

'ARO SA' started making automotive parts in the 1950s with their first complete car rolling off the Campulung Muscel production line in 1957. The 'IMS 57' was also the first off-road vehicle produced in Romania, but in 1966 design work began on a new 4 x 4 vehicle. The first production 'ARO 240' series appeared in 1971 and around 125,000 original and later specification variants have been built up to 2004. Many of them have been exported not

could be found everywhere between the Baltic and the Black Sea. In recent years the author observed examples in Lithuania on the non-forestry Panevezys to Anyksciai line as well as in Ukraine on the Vygoda Forestry Railway and the state-owned Borzhava Valley Agricultural Railway (a part of which is now operated by a forestry combine at Dovge). These modern speeders carry up to four people and their tools, offering a scooter-like protection against the elements for their riders. In order to change the direction of travel the crew lifts the vehicle from the track, turns it around and lowers it again. Readers familiar with British railway practice will

The Felsötarkany Forestry Railway in the Bükk Mountains may be one of the shortest forestry lines in Hungary but it is certainly the best maintained and friendliest! Upon the author's visit the manager of the line arranged a demonstration of the line's little draisine - which apparently can be lifted from the track and rotated by its crew using a built-in turntable. Motor and transmission parts of this locally assembled lightweight 'pet' came from an East German 'Trabant', yielding a rocket-like acceleration! (24.08.2003).

Right and below: A handle is inserted to jack down the little turntable and lift the vehicle up off the rails. The performance of turning the car round attracts a great deal of attention.

Below: The unique Hungarian draisine is ready for a trip.

only to East European countries but also to Western Europe. The popular 'ARO 240' and its variants often served as a basis for several locally designed draisines. Its popularity as a railcar is certainly due to its solid construction. In contrast to ordinary cars off-road vehicles are usually built on a ladder frame that adds rigidity to the construction.

One heavily rebuilt example can be seen on the Lillafüred Forestry Railway in Hungary, based on a four-door 'ARO 244' version. At Majlath motive power depot the car was adapted for use on the 760 mm gauge rails with the shortening of the front and

the addition of a new underframe and boot. The resulting railcar - designated 'S02-119' is currently stored out of use at Majlath although back in Romania a less heavily rebuilt example of the 'ARO 244' is still operational on the Vișeu de Sus Forestry Railway.

Like standard gauge Czech 'Škoda' railcar conversions - based on saloon and estate body styles, several examples of the original 'Škoda 1201' (and its successor, the model '1202') have also been observed on Czech and Slovak narrow gauge forestry railways. One well-restored example still exists at Čierny Balog, on the 760 mm gauge Čiernohronská Lesná Železnica. It is a 'Škoda 1202 STW' estate, produced between 1963 and 1971. As can be seen from the accompanying picture, it received a completely new underframe with central link and pin coupling. The couplings at both ends make it possible to haul light unpowered trolleys or to convey the railcar at the rear of an ordinary train.

Bucegis and TVs: custom-built lorries and vans on rails

Romanian forestry railways have in particular possessed a large number of lorries on rails. A number of these have survived in serviceable condition on the Vișeu de Sus forestry railway, still fulfilling a variety of tasks. The lorries not only carry the maintenance staff and their equipment to construction sites. Fitted with coupling gear they can even haul one or two empty flat cars or perform shunting duties when required. Due to their light weight when compared with steam locomotives, they can negotiate worn-out track or track damaged by flooding, i.e. circumstances where the use of locomotives would be impossible. Another advantage of this kind of draisine is their speed. They are several times faster than a steam train.

In most cases these vehicles were converted from lorries built by the 'Steagul Rosu' ('Red Flag') plant at Brasov in the Carpathians, the former 'Astra' ('Star') company. Starting in 1960 'Steagul Rosu' built two types of lorries, the 'SR-131 Carpati' with a payload of three tons and the 'SR-113 Bucegi' with a payload of five tons. While the meaning of "Carpati" should be clear, the name 'Bucegi' refers to the Bucegi Plateau, which is part of the Southern Carpathians. Today the 'SR-113' is the most widely used rail-lorry in Romania. In the conversion process its underframe was reinforced and a four-wheel bogie was placed under the front of the vehicle. The torque from the V8 petrol engine is transmitted via a cardan shaft to the single rear axle while a turntable has been fitted under the centre of gravity. This can be cranked down to the top of the rails, after which a few more manual revolutions are needed to lift the lorry clear of the rails so that it can be turned around by hand. Turning the steering wheel, which is in its usual place, will actuate the brake shoes fitted to the bogie.

Another product of the Romanian automotive industry has been the 'TV' delivery van. The designation may sound a little curious to the foreigner, but 'TV' are the initials of Tudor Vladimirescu, a well-known folk hero (at least in Romania...), who gave his name to the manufacturing plant. The conversion followed the same principles as outlined above.

On the Vișeu de Sus forestry railway at least three versions of the 'TV' delivery van have been converted for rail use. A 'TV' with an unaltered interior was used to carry workers, another example was used as an ambulance, while the Romanian police used a cream 'TV-41' for patrol duties along the border with Ukraine, which is only a few hundred metres away in one place.

In recent years an influx of western technology has led to the

Among several other pieces of railway equipment this well-restored 'Škoda' draisine stands in front of the engine shed of the Čiernohronská Lesní Dráha at Čierny Balog in Slovakia. It originally left the Škoda car factory in Mladá Boleslav as a type '1202 STW', the sedan version of this popular Czech car. The draisine in front is a narrow gauge adaptation of a standard gauge Tatra service vehicle (30.08.2003).

Right: Čierny Balog's Škoda estate car stands near the station with a 4-wheel passenger coach in tow. In the background is the railway's former diesel railcar, M21.006 which, with it's motor long gone, has been restored as a buffet car.

The Vişeu de Sus Forestry Railway in Northern Romania is a mecca for those who like lorries and vans on rails. A large number of vehicles of both types are in use, probably no two of them looking exactly alike! Many have been rebuilt from the Romanian 'SR-131 Bucegi' 3-ton lorry such as this example and another overleaf, both operated by R.G. Holz. In the conversion process under-frames are reinforced and a four-wheel bogie placed under the front of the lorry.

Another 'SR-131 Bucegi' 5-ton lorry on the Vişeu de Sus Forestry Railway, its chassis strengthened and modified for railway use and fitted with couplings. As the sign indicates, it is now operated by the RG Holz Company. (26.08.2003).

introduction of draisines based on fairly new non-Romanian vans. At Vişeu de Sus at least one German Volkswagen van of the square-fronted 'T3' series and a 'Mercedes-Benz' van of type '206 D', '207 D' or '208 D' (which are all externally the same) have been set up for operation over the 760 mm gauge tracks. As the 'Mercedes-Benz' operated by the forestry department is quite a large vehicle there is space enough inside to carry the half dozen foresters and their gear for a trip into the mountains.

GMDs and others:
the unified factory-built variety

Starting in 1950/1951 the Russian Demihovo Machine Works (which produced other narrow gauge rolling stock as well),

Still on the Vişeu de Sus Forestry Railway, we illustrate two versions of the classic Romanian 'TV' delivery van converted for railway use. The one pictured above was used by the Romanian police for border patrols while the blue one on the left was used as workers transportation and is largely unaltered except for the modifications necessary to mount it on the railway. (26.08.2003).

Right and below: Certainly the most modern draisines in Romania are those that have been converted from the German 'Volkswagen' and 'Mercedes-Benz' vans. The largest specimen must be this recently rebuilt green 'Mercedes-Benz' of type '206 D', '207 D' or '208 D', which can carry a full crew of foresters and their equipment (26.08.2003).

Below: If you see a VW 'camper' in Cornwall it's normally carrying surf boards on the roof. In Romania things are a little different. This Volkswagen T3 is in use on the Vişeu de Sus Forestry Railway (the so-called Water Valley Railway). It was photographed by Moritz Heintze on August 7th, 2002.

the Kaluga Engineering Works (which has also produced broad-gauge diesel shunters for the Soviet State Railways and industrial railways in the USSR) and the car manufacturer 'ZIL' produced several versions of both two and three-axle draisines (according to one source the Kaluga Engineering Works were the sole producer). In their construction many components of the popular 'GAZ-51' lorry were incorporated: especially the long bonnet and the cab. Production lasted well into the 1960s and draisines of this type were delivered not only to the forestry railways but also to public and industrial narrow gauge railways within the Soviet Union. Today the last working examples can be found in Ukraine, while several non-operational vehicles are in the large collection of the Lavassaare narrow gauge railway museum in Estonia (the latter mainly coming from industrial railways).

Some of the oldest surviving draisines have been preserved as part of the large collection at the Lavassaare narrow gauge railway museum in Estonia. The pictures show a cosmetically-restored 'GMD-1' goods draisine and an example of the 'PD-1' version: a passenger draisine with the dimensions of a small railcar. These factory-built draisines differ from the locally-built types in Romania in having a rigid front axle and a powered bogie at the rear (15.08.2001).

The goods draisines were designated 'GMD-1', 'GMD-2' and 'GMD-4', with the letters 'MD' standing for motor draisine and the letter 'G' standing for their purpose, the carrying of goods. During the long period of construction their appearance was altered when the 'GAZ-51' was "face-lifted" and thus the "Dash" versions came into being. The 'PD-1' version (with no 'M' in the middle…!) can best be described as the passenger draisine (albeit having almost the dimensions of a small railcar). Like the goods version it has three axles, the front axle being a rigid non-driven axle and the two at the rear forming a powered bogie, thus differing from the Romanian draisines. Other versions have been the 'SMD-1' ambulance draisine and the 'PMD-1' fire engine on rails.

On Ukrainian forestry railways the widespread use of draisines considerably reduced the need for loco-hauled trains. On most railways a heavy train with bogie flat cars or trucks only rarely left the shed for their loading points more than once or twice a week. During the working week draisines would make many runs to supply the workers or to perform light shunting duties.

On the Bieszcadzka Kolejka Lesna at Cisna in Poland a draisine of very different appearance was in use. The vehicle was series-built by PKP in their own workshops, most likely in Krosniewice or Koronowo. Its official designation is 'Wmc' ('Wm' standing for motor vehicle, 'c' for 'petrol engine' instead of 'd' for 'diesel engine'). These vehicles use engines and transmissions from popular Polish post-war cars, like the 'Syrena' (the car being somewhat similar to the 'Wartburg' built in the GDR) and the 'Zuk/Nysa' (a family of light vans based on the Russian 'GAZ-M20').

At least until recently the 'Wmc' at Cisna could be hired by small groups of tourists for trips into the Bieszczady Mountains, a practice also well-known on Ukrainian forestry railways, where draisines are used to carry berry pickers into the woods.

A look into the future: railways for pleasure?

It is likely that the era of forestry railways will be drawing to a close in the very near future. As mentioned above several forestry railways, especially those in Hungary, now rely on hikers and tourists which they carry into the woods. On these railways draisines will have a chance to be used well into the 21st century for their original purposes. Upon a visit to the Lithuanian Panevezys - Anyksciai narrow gauge railway, which closed down for regular traffic at the end of 2001, the author observed speeders towing light pushcars fitted with benches and some weather protection over the 750 mm gauge tracks in the Lithuanian hills.

The author is fully aware of the fact, that his work is far from being complete and that he could describe only a fraction of the many home-built vehicles that have been running through the Carpathian Mountains.

Although constructed much later, the 'GMD-2' of the Vygoda Forestry Railway in Ukraine was built to the same principles as the older Soviet goods draisines. This is the probably the last surviving (and still working!) example. It was photographed at Myndunok Solotvynskyj (28.08.2003).

The Vygoda Forestry Railway's lorry stands beside a forester's house whose architecture is typical of buildings in the area, including the railway stations. In many ways the scene is not so different to that of some American short lines that once operated 'Galloping Goose' lorries and which are popular with modellers.

On the Bieszcadzka Kolejka Lesna at Cisna in South Eastern Poland a single draisine of the 'Wmc' type is in use, which, at least until recently, could be hired by small groups of tourists for trips into the Bieszczady Mountains. Built by the PKP workshops it incorporated several automotive parts (29.08.2003).

The Lithuanian Panevezys - Anyksciai narrow gauge railway closed down for regular traffic at the end of 2001. An attempt was made shortly before to use the infrastructure for operating light speeders towing light trailers. This photo shows the draisines in front of Anyksciai station (which houses a small museum on the history of the line) (18.08.2001).

A close up of the Panevezys - Anyksciai railway speeder at the line's terminus at Rubikiai.

Sources:

Aleš Kucera and Aleš Bilek: Karpatské Lesní Železnice (Carpathian Forestry Railways) Konting spol. s.r.o., Nachod 2003

Wolfram Wendelin: Karpatendampf Band 1, Schmalspurbahnen in Ostgalizien
(Steam in the Carpathians Vol. 1, Narrow Gauge Railways in Eastern Galicia) published by the author, 2002

Helmuth Lampeitl: Schmalspurbahnen in der Ukraine, Bahn im Bild 113 (Narrow Gauge in Ukraine, Railways in Pictures Vol. 113) Verlag Peter Pospischil, Vienna 2000

Mehis Helme: Raudteemuuseum Lavassaare (Estonian Museum Railway Lavassaare) published by the museum, 1995

Alfred B. Gottwaldt: Autos auf Schienen (Cars on Wheels) Franckh'sche Verlagshandlung, Stuttgart 1986

All photos by the author - except where credited.

Diesels and Electrics in Eskişehir, Turkey *by Paul Catchpole*

Tülomsaş, the Türkiye Lokomotif ve Motor Sanayii A. Ş., is the largest and most modern locomotive and wagon works in the Middle East and supplies railways through out the region as well as in Turkey. Work for the TCDD (Türkiye Cumhuriyeti Devlet Demiryollari) includes overhauls as well as new construction. In this view in the erecting hall DE 22.075 is being craned over to newly painted bogies and has an overhauled 16-cylinder 1580 kW diesel engine awaiting installation. Tülomsaş built 86 examples of the DE 22 under licence from General Motors, the class corresponding to GM type G26CW-2. (Some further history and information about Tülomsaş is scheduled for a future publication on railways in Turkey).

E43.013 is one of 45 25kV Bo-Bo-Bo electric locomotives supplied to the TCDD by Tülomsaş and Toshiba from 1987. When the first suburban lines were electrified the poles were spaced further apart than later on and so to allow for a greater deflection from the rail centre line on curves, wider current collectors were required. As a result, an unusual feature of these locos is that one of the pantographs is larger than the other for working over the older electrified sections.

In the 1960s and 1970s Končar of Zagreb built some Bo-Bo electrics under licence from ASEA of Sweden (SJ type Rb). The TCDD hired some renovated examples of the former JZ class 441 from Bosnia-Herzegovinia in 1998, and later purchased a total of 20 locos, including those which had been on hire. E 52.516 heading west is one of these. Renovation was undertaken by the builder in Croatia in line with the HZ class 1141.3.

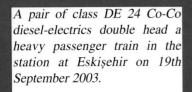

A pair of class DE 24 Co-Co diesel-electrics double head a heavy passenger train in the station at Eskişehir on 19th September 2003.

Left: Eskişehir shed used to be known for its large Prussian-style 4-8-0s but today the DE 24 is the most common locomotive type to be found at the depot. In this view the part-roundhouse hosts DE 24.314, DE 24.384 and an unidentified member of the class, plus several locos inside.

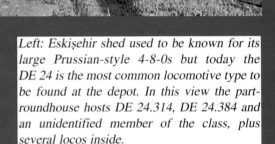

DE 24.335 and DE 24.348, wearing the typical red and white livery of diesel-electric locomotives, receive attention at the back of the former steam shed. The plates illustrated inset are from the cabside of DE 24.314, shown above.

Diesel hydraulic Bo-Bo no. DH 9524 acting as station pilot at Eskişehir in September 2003. Tülomsaş built 26 locos of this type in 1999 as a variant of the class DE 11, incorporating an hydraulic transmission instead of electrical. The 700kW/950hp power rating and 80 km/h maximum speed define this as a shunting and trip freight locomotive, the engine installed being a type MTU 8V 396 TC 13.

A special thanks is due for the friendly courtesy of TCDD and Tülomsaş staff in enabling these photographs to be taken.

The Soviet class TU3 and Czechoslovakian class TU47 Narrow Gauge Diesel Locomotives *by Paul Engelbert*

In the mid-1950s Českomoravská-Kolben-Daněk (ČKD) from Prague in Czechoslovakia developed a diesel electric locomotive for the narrow gauge lines of the Czechoslovak State Railways (ČSD). This type was later also exported to the Soviet Union. This article reviews the interesting history of this first larger series of narrow gauge main line diesel locomotives in Eastern Europe.

The Czechoslovak class TU47

In late 1954 and early 1955 ČKD delivered the first batch of six class TU47 with works numbers 2944 through 2949. The ČSD initially numbered them T47.001 through T47.006, later changing the prefix from 'T' to 'TU', the U signifying 'uzkorozchodný', meaning narrow gauge.

The class TU47 is a Bo'Bo' diesel electric locomotive with a power of 350 hp and a maximum speed of 40 km/h. The total weight of a TU47 is 30.5 tons; the axle load 7.6 tons. Technically the TU47 is based on proven technology, but this was its first use in this combination on a narrow gauge locomotive. The new narrow gauge locomotive was fitted with the same type of diesel engine already used in the ČSD's class M262.0 standard gauge railcars and the electric traction motors were of the same type as used in tramcars.

The body of the locomotive is quite long: 12 metres. This length iss visually strengthened by the small bogies, low platework and the integral snowplough. The body was divided into four compartments: a cabin, an engine room, a luggage compartment and the second cabin.

The locos were delivered in a striking red livery with white lining and a white stripe, accentuating the round streamlined shapes of the cabs. The roof, the bogies and the integral snow-plough were grey and the couplings black. A round metal plate with the ČKD logo was mounted on the front of the loco, right

TU3-002 at Lavassaare Museum on 15th August 2002 displays the front-end design of the class in its traditional red livery with white lining and with the ČKD builder's plate affixed below the white outline of a red star flanked by cast numbers.

Photo: Paul Engelbert.

ČD loco 705.905 from the first series at Nová Bystrice on 25th June 1993, still carrying the ČSD logo six months after the 'velvet divorce' of the Czech and Slovak states and with the older number, TU47.005 painted on the front. Comparison with locos supplied to the USSR and later ČSD batches shows that the first series had smaller louvres and no cabin door at the near end on the visible side.

Photo: Paul Engelbert.

above the coupling. Another plate with the works number was mounted on the side of the loco. Soon after they had been taken into service a large red star with a white outline was painted on the front of the locos, above the ČKD plate.

All six engines were allocated to the Jindřichův Hradec depot in Southern Bohemia. Four of them were scrapped in the late 1970s and early 1980s so only TU47.005 and 006, now renumbered 705.905 and 705.906, are still at Jindřichův Hradec. Noticeably 705.905 has not been in service since 2001 but is due to be overhauled and modernised.

The modified design for the USSR

The class TU47 proved to be successful and hence ČKD tried to sell more of these engines. Because there

were no modern narrow gauge diesel locomotives in Eastern Europe or in the Soviet Union, the market potential for a locomotive such as the class TU47 was enormous. Unfortunately for ČKD the Russian Kaluga factory also tried to fill this gap with its own class TU2 diesel locomotive (produced 1955-1959).

For the narrow gauge lines in the Soviet Union ČKD developed a slightly modified version of the Czechoslovak class TU47. This was the Soviet class TU3 (Ty3 in Cyrillic). Originally the Soviet Union is said to have ordered 200 locomotives.

The most important modification was the gear ratio of the axle reducers of the traction motors. This was altered from 15:82 to 15:85 in order to increase the maximum speed from 40 to 50 km/h. Furthermore, the ventilation system was modified, resulting in larger ventilation louvres on both sides of the engine. Additionally, a normal hinged door replaced the folding door of the luggage compartment.

Eventually the total weight of the class TU3 was 32 tons, resulting in an axle load of 8 tons, but the general appearance of the class TU3 did not differ much from the Czechoslovak class TU47. The typical streamlined shape of the cabs, the red livery with white stripes and the star on the front of the locos were retained.

The class TU3 was quite luxurious, especially compared to her Russian counterpart; the class TU2 diesel locomotive. Ventilators switched on automatically, they had a good signalling system, reliable speed indicators and the noise level inside the locomotive was very low. A special feature of the class TU3 was the sleeping compartment next to one of the cabs, which was equipped with a table, a bed and a locker. It was intended for personnel accompanying freight trains.

The class TU3 was designed for one-man operation. In case the engine driver lost vigilance, the locomotive would automatically make an emergency brake application. The control console could be controlled both from the left-hand side and from the right hand side, so the engine driver could move around freely around the cabin. During shunting operations especially this was very practical. Noticeably the most comfortable way for the driver to operate these locomotives was standing, not sitting. Folding seats were however available for the engine driver. It was also possible to operate two class TU3 from one cab in accordance with the multiple-unit system.

In 1957 ČKD delivered the first batch of ten class TU3 with works numbers 3909 through 3918. They received running numbers TU3-001 through TU3-010. The first trial runs with TU3-001 were conducted on the

A more complete view of Lavassaare Museum's loco, TU3-002 in its original livery. Photo: Paul Engelbert.

Jindřichův Hradec network in May 1957. After the first locomotives had been exported to the Soviet Union, the Central Scientific Research Institute of the MPS in Shatura also tested the class TU3. Further trial runs were conducted with TU3-001 and TU3-002, which both turned up on the Tumskaya network near Moscow in 1957.

In 1958 series production commenced at ČKD, starting with TU3-011 (works number 4110). In the same year though, the order was cancelled. In the end, only 45 class TU3 locomotives were built. The last locomotive is TU3-045 with works number 4144.

In 1961 additional speed trials were scheduled. For this purpose TU3-001 and TU3-003, accompanied by engineers from ČKD, were transferred to the Panevežys network in Lithuania. The

trial runs were conducted on the Panevežys - Joniškelis section, which has almost no curves or gradients. During the tests the locos reached speeds of up to 80 km/h.

The short life of the class TU3

Judging by the numbers produced of classes TU2 (281) and class TU3 (45), it can be concluded that the high-tech class TU3 could not compete with the simple Russian-built class TU2. Maybe the class TU3 was simply too luxurious for the simple needs of narrow gauge lines in the Soviet Union? In any case the price of a TU3 will most probably have been higher than that of a TU2, though given the relationship of the USSR to Czechoslovakia, it is doubtful whether the Soviets paid the full market price for them.

Anyway, the price was probably not the deciding factor. The reason why the Soviet Ministry of Transport (MPS) did not adopt the class TU3 on a large scale is - in hindsight - a shortcoming in the basic design of the locomotive. Due to its long length it can only be used on lines with a minimum curve radius of 70 m, whereas 750-mm gauge railways generally have sharper curves. At least this applies for the narrow gauge lines in the Soviet Union, so for most lines the class TU3 was not even an option. It should be noted incidentally that the narrow gauge lines in Czechoslovakia, for which the TU47 was originally designed, all have a large minimum curve radius.

Another factor probably influenc-

Close up of the bogie detail, also showing the ČKD Sokolov, Praga plate on TU3-002. Photo: Paul Engelbert.

ing the decision not to use many class TU3 is a political one. Instead of importing locomotives from Czechoslovakia, the Soviets could build class TU2 locomotives in their own country. Also spare parts had to be imported from Czechoslovakia for the TU3. This not only influenced the decision to buy the locomotives from ČKD, in fact, this might have been one of the reasons for taking the class TU3 out of service after only a few years.

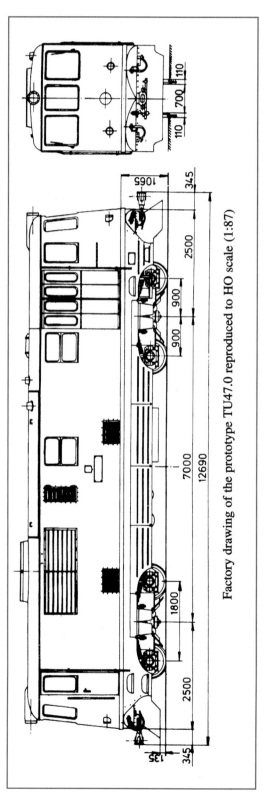

Factory drawing of the prototype TU47.0 reproduced to HO scale (1:87)

In 1968 the national uprising against the Communist regime took place in Czechoslovakia. Although the Soviets suppressed the uprising, relations between Czechoslovakia and the Soviet Union were badly disturbed. The supply of spare parts for the class TU3 declined, allegedly, as a result of the changed political climate. The depots and workshops had more and more difficulties in maintaining the class TU3, thus the Soviets decided to replace the Czech locomotives with Russian class TU2s which had become superfluous due to the closure of narrow gauge lines in other parts of the Soviet Union.

Reports of class TU3 working in the Soviet Union

Because the class TU3 was soon taken out of service, there is little information available about the whereabouts of the 45 engines of this class. Not even half the locos (22 out of a total of 45) could be identified.

The most important location where the class TU3 was used is the Panevežys system in Lithuania, a public railway operated by the MPS. Fourteen TU3s were used here between 1961 and 1970 carrying running numbers 001 - 003 and 033 - 043. They were the backbone of the motive power on this extensive system. The class TU2s also allocated to Panevežys MPD stood in reserve, with the TU3s doing most of the work. Between 1965 and 1973 the TU3 fleet was gradually replaced by TU2s from Estonia and Northern-Kazakhstan.

Another MPS network probably using the class TU3 was the Gajvoron system in the Ukraine. Older staff at the depot have confirmed that some TU3s had been in Gajvoron for a short period of time. All locos disappeared before 1961. Czech railway staff from the Osoblaha system report having seen two TU3s double heading a freight train in the Kiev Region many years ago. It is unclear exactly which railway was observed, the MPS system based at Gajvoron or the Chervonoje sugar beet railway? According to Ukrainian railway enthusiasts, some TU3 have worked at Chervonoje. The Chervonoje sugar railway used to be connected to the Gajvoron network. This leads to the hypothesis, that the TU3s from Gajvoron had been transferred to Chervonoje.

At least 14 class TU3s have run on various industrial railways in Russia, Latvia and the Ukraine. Only seven of these engines could be identified: TU3-004 worked at the cement factory in Brotseni (Latvia). In 1962 it was transferred to the Struzhany peat railway. TU3-025 was allocated to the forestry railways of Urensky (1959-1960) and Viksunsky (1960-1978), both in Russia. The following two engines, TU3-026 and 027, remained together. They worked on the Russian forestry railways of Kirovsky and Redkino and later on the peat railway of Karinskoe. TU3-017 also worked on the Redkino forestry railway between 1958 and 1968. TU3-044 and 045 formed another couple. Between 1959 and 1972 they worked on the Teresva forestry railway in the Ukraine.

The other seven engines working on industrial railways could not be identified by their running numbers. The forestry railways of Vygoda (Ukraine) and Alapaevsk (Russia) as well as the Fosforitny industrial railway (Russia) are reported to have had at least one class TU3 in stock. The Verhie-Ufalejsk industrial system in Russia even had a fleet of four unknown class TU3s.

Today fourteen engines cannot be accounted for. Some of them are likely to have been been running at Gajvoron and Chervonoje. Others probably worked on isolated industrial railways, unnoticed by the outside world. Maybe they even worked on the Virgin Lands development railways in northern Kazakhstan? At least one engine (TU3-024) has turned up at the grain elevator in Atbasar in northern Kazakhstan. But were there more TU3s here? It will probably not be possible to completely resolve this mystery after so many years.

The TU3s originally running at Panevežys were intended to be transferred to a forestry railway on the Isle of Sakhalin, but it is unclear whether they ever arrived there, because all but three of Panevežys's TU3s have turned up on pioneer railways. Second-hand TU3s from Panevežys were used on the pioneer railways of St. Petersburg, Novomoskovsk, Lutsk, Ľvov, Donetsk, Rovno, Uzhgorod and Riga.

Riga's TU3-035 was later transferred to the Tbilisi pioneer railway in Georgia but it was never used there for a familiar reason: the curve radius of this pioneer railway was to small for the class TU3.

On pioneer railways the class TU3 was not used very intensively, so the need for spare parts was low. In the 1970s and 1980s, however, most pioneer railways replaced their TU3s with TU2s or even with modern TU7s.

The last pioneer railway using the class TU3 is the one in Ľvov in the Ukraine. Here TU3-039 is still in active service. Its last overhaul dates from 30th April 2003. This is the last locomotive of this class in working order. It normally runs on Wednesdays and Thusdays from May until September. Until 1998 TU3-040 also worked on the Lvov pioneer railway. TU3-001 of the St.Petersburg pioneer railway has been standing in reserve since 1996 and is probably not operational any more. A further two TU3s have been preserved, one in the Lavassaare railway museum in Estonia (TU3-002) and the other at Alexandrin, near Rovno in the Ukraine (TU3-034). Neither are operational.

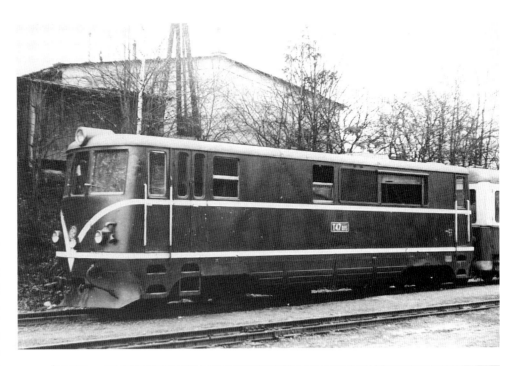

Czech loco T47.015 from the second series of ČSD locos pictured at Jindřichův Hradec in southern Bohemia in 1968, still then carrying the original number plate without the 'U'. Note also the position of the horns on the front of the cab instead of on the roof.

Photo: archive of Václav Polívka.

The modified class TU47 in Czechoslovakia

The Czechoslovak State Railways also ordered 15 examples of the modified class TU47 diesel locomotive in 1958. These were almost exactly identical to the Soviet class TU3. The only known difference is the door of the luggage compartment.

The first batch of ten locos had works numbers 4087 - 4096 and the second batch of five locos were 4145 - 4149. It is said that the locos from the second batch were originally intended to be exported to the Soviet Union.

Despite the noticeable technical differences, the ČSD considered these modified locomotives to be of the same type as the six diesel locomotives built in 1954-1955 (TU47.001 - TU47.006). Hence these modified engines were numbered TU47.007 through TU47.021.

Contrary to their Russian sisters, the modified class TU47 only ran on public railways operated by the Czechoslovakian State Railways. The original distribution was as follows:

Frýdlant (750-mm gauge):	TU47.007, 008, 009, 010
Jindřichův Hradec:	TU47.011, 012, 015
Osoblaha:	TU47.013, 014, 016, 017
Ružomberok (Slovakia):	TU47.018, 019, 020, 021

Most TU47s had a gauge of 760 mm and were equipped with Bosna couplings but the engines allocated to Frýdlant had a gauge of 750 mm and were fitted with a central buffer. It was possible to convert the gauge of the locomotives between 750 mm and 760 mm. Most of Frýdlant's TU47s now run on the 760 mm gauge

system at Jindřichův Hradec. Conversely the original 760 mm gauge engines TU47.019 and 020 temporarily ran on the 750 mm Frýdlant system.

Nowadays the narrow gauge lines of Frýdlant and Ružomberok are closed and the class TU47 only works from the Osoblaha and Jindřichův Hradec MPDs. They are almost the only motive power on these remaining narrow gauge lines in the Czech Republic. In 2003 12 out of 15 engines from the second TU47 series were still present in a more or less working order: TU47.013, 014, 016 and 017 running on the ČD line Osoblaha - Tremešna. TU47.007, 011, 012, 015, 018, 019, 020 and 021 meanwhile work on the privatised Jindřichův Hradec network, opereted by the JHMD.

On both lines the class TU47 has officially been renumbered as class 705.9 (for instance TU47.007 became 705.907). The number plates on the sides of the engines all show these new numbers, but often the original TU47 number is still painted on the front of the locomotive.

The crashed TU47.012 alias 705.912 was rebuilt by the JHMD in 2002 using parts from other crashed locos. It has been equipped with a new LIAZ M640C diesel engine. 705.915 has also been fitted with the new engine and modernised electronic equipment. In 2003 the Czech state railways similarly rebuilt their 705.917. As a result of the modifications the fuel consumption decreased by 50%. Unfortunately 705.915 has hit been by a tractor since being remotored and requires some expensive repairs.

The Czech engines were originally painted in the same red livery as the Russian TU3 but since the 1980s the TU47s have been repainted in new liveries over and over again. Nowadays it is hard to find two engines in the same livery. The basic colours used are red, orange or blue, mixed with different types of white and yellow stripe. It is nice to see some engines again running in their original red livery with white stripes.

705.911-6, formerly TU47.011, pulls into the narrow gauge terminus at Jindřichův Hradec in April 1997. The loco has been restored to the early livery but without either ČSD or ČD logos, nor yet with the JHMD logo - and definitely no red star!   Photo: Paul Catchpole.

their eyes on the DDR. Especially in Saxony, not far from the location of the ČKD factory, there were many hundreds of kilometres of 750 mm gauge local railways. These lines were all steam operated.

Indeed, the East German State Railway (DR) was interested in diesel locomotives for their narrow gauge lines. Negotiations resulted in plans to import an unknown number of locomotives of roughly the same type as the class TU3 at the end of 1961. At first trial runs were scheduled on the line from Freital-Hainsberg to Kurort Kipsdorf. but then it turned out that in different stations along the line there were dozens of points with a radius of 65 metres. This circumstance made it impossible for class TU3 diesel engines to run on the line, for they require a minimum curve radius of 70 metres and would get stuck or derail at the points. Hence the trial runs could not proceed as planned and the ČKD did not get the order.

Export plans to the DDR

Because the plan to export locomotives to the Soviet Union failed, ČKD searched for other export customers. The factory laid

TECHNICAL DATA AND COMPARISON OF TU47 AND TU3 PRODUCTION VARIANTS			
Technical details	**TU47.001 - 006**	**TU3-001 - 045**	**TU47.007 - 015**
Length of body	12,000 mm		
Length over couplings	12,690 mm	12,730 mm (750 mm)	12,690 mm (760 mm)
Wdith of body	2422 mm		
Height above the rail	3325 mm	3370 mm	
Axle formula	Bo'Bo'		
Wheel base	1800 mm		
Distance between bogie pins	7000 mm		
Weight	30.5 t	32 t	
Axle load	7.63 t	8.0 t	
Gauge	760 mm	750 mm	760 mm
Wheel diameter	760 mm		
Minimum curve radius	70 m		
Type of motor	ČKD 12V170DR; Diesel; V-12 configuration		
Revolutions per minute	1250		
Power output	350 HP (295 kW)		
Fuel consumption	70 kg/h		
Power output generator	257 kW		
Rated power / motor	46 kW (420V x 110A)		
Number of motors	4		
Revolutions per minute	650		
Gear ratio	15 : 82	15 : 85	
Maximum speed	40 km/h	50 km/h	
Maximum thrust	6.6 t	9.0 t	
	(at 26.2 km/h)	(at 15 km/h)	

Some Electric Veterans in South America   *by Günter Koch*

"Dig out those odd shots" (of diesels and electrics, that is) "taken on steam bashes abroad", was the editor's call in Locomotives International issue 65. Well that's what I did, and the result presented here is exactly to the editor's definition: a loose sequence of "odd" but certainly no "master" shots, with no system and absolutely no claim to completeness, taken when an electric engine accidentally passed by instead of the beloved steam so much searched for. Yet I hope those photos may be of some interest, especially as electric railways are rather a rarity in South America.

BRAZIL

Let me start with Brazil as the majority of my photographs come from that country, for two reasons. Firstly, the largest country on the South American continent has (or at least had) the largest share of electrified lines and secondly, in the 1970s I went to Brazil several times for professional reasons, doing teaching and consulting work at research institutions. In 1978 my allocation was at São Paulo and I used weekends and vacation days especially for seeing as much as possible of steam operations which then still existed. My guide was that grand "World of South American Steam" by Roy Christian and Ken Mills which I had accidentally found at a Cologne book shop two years earlier (I was still in my "railway infancy" at this time and had little knowledge of such exotic areas), and my Brazilian hosts were great in making contacts for official visits to railways and factories. I also made the acquaintance of Patric Dollinger, the founder and first president of the Brazilian ABPF, and I wish to take this occasion to bring back his memory. I remember him as a most active promoter of railway preservation and as a most knowledgeable advisor to visiting guests. His tragic death in 1985, following a car accident suffered in the USA, was a sad loss for the international community.

The photo on the front cover of Co-Co locomotive No. 1000 of the E.F. Santos a Jundiaí was taken at Paranapiacaba on 19th October 1978 when I visited the famous inclines down the Serra do Mar to Piassaguera. It was one of those "official" visits mentioned above and I was splendidly received by Sr. Agostinho Quilici, shed master at Paranapiacaba, who showed me all his installations and gave me a ride on loco-brake No. 8 down and up the "Serra Nova", or New Incline, then still in regular operation. When red-livened No. 1000 arrived on a freight train I just found the time for a typical "odd shot". That this locomotive was of historic significance did not come to my mind, but it was indeed the first electric locomotive supplied to the

former São Paulo Railway when its main line was electrified from Paranapiacaba via São Paulo to Jundiaí in 1949/50. As it was often the case, there was no time to look for builder's plates which were anyway often not carried, hence most of the identifications given in this article are based on Reg Carter's "Railways of Brazil" lists. No. 1000 was built by English Electric, No. 1779/1949, as the first of a series of 16. Its "Long-nose" streamlining, antique as it may appear today, is typical of the period. Gauge 5'3" (1600 mm). Current 3000 V d.c. Power 3000 hp (2240 kW).

B-B rack locomotive No. 2001 of the same railway, which I photographed on the same occasion, below) could certainly not be called a "veteran" in 1978, as it had been built by Hitachi just five years earlier, nevertheless a close-up look which reveals some of its unique technology may not cone amiss. The "Serra Velha' (Old Incline) which had been completely reconstructed as a rack line with a 3-bar Abt rack and overhead catenary of 3000 V d.c., had started operating in 1973. At first it was plagued with teething troubles but by 1978 these had been overcome and the railway was working smoothly, with the effect that the beautiful Serra Nova rope incline was close to the end of its days.

The locomotives, always operating in pairs, work on the rack-and-adhesion principle. Each of the two four-wheel bogies has two vertically adjustable pinions which are lowered on the rack section but raised on the short level sections at each end of the incline, in order to avoid collision with rails on switches, crossings etc. Each pinion has its own motor while the four bogie wheels are driven by a single motor via a jackshaft drive, clearly visible in in the photo below. The locomotive thus has six traction motors, each rated at 463 kW (630 metric hp), or a total output of

Hitachi B-B rack loco no. 2001 at Paranapiacaba on 19th October 1978.

131-ton 1Co-Co1s on the metre gauge at Sorocabana, no. 2003 nearest.

130 tons, built by General Electric and Westinghouse. The photo adjacent shows No. 2003 (GE 13106/1943) in front of one of her sisters. Both the FEPASA and the RFFSA have recently been privatised but the new owners found the equipment of most electrified lines in a seriously run-down state of repair. As a consequence the current has been turned off on all Brazilian main lines and electric traction replaced by diesel, with the sole exception of the Serra Velha rack line mentioned earlier. Electric traction remains on urban transport systems including metro lines, most of which have been taken over by local public companies.

2780 kW. Wheel diameter 1120 mm. Length 16,760 mm. Mass 188 t. Speed 38 km/h on rack / 45 km/h on adhesion sections. Tractive force (one hour) 378 kN (85,000 lb).

The British-owned São Paulo Railway had come under Federal State control in 1948 and hence was included in the Federal RFFSA system when formed in 1957. Most other railways in the State of São Paulo were, however, taken over by the local railway administration FEPASA, an abbreviation of Ferrovias Paulistas S.A. Its main constituents were the broad-gauge Paulista and Araraquara railways, and the metre gauge Sorocabana and Mogiana systems. A visit to Sorocaba on Oct. 1st 1978, gave an opportunity to stroll through the station and yard of the former E.F. Sorocabana, and as it was a Sunday not much was working and many locomotives were lying idle at home. The Sorocabana had started electrifying its main line with 3000 V d.c. in 1943, with huge locomotives of the 1-Co-Co-1 type weighing

A short private metre gauge railway called the Estrada de Ferro Electrica Votorantim (EFEV) ran from Sorocaba to the town of Votorantim and onwards to Santa Elena, a distance of roughly 15 km, where the large Votoran Cement Factory was located. Both the railway and the plant were owned by the same company and the main duty for the railway was to transport bagged cement to the Sorocabana and supplies to the factory. The railway had originally been built to the 600 mm gauge but in 1920 was converted to metre and electrified with 500 V d.c. Three nice little 40-ton Bo-Bo electric locomotives were received from General Electric in 1946 and a fourth one followed a decade later. The railway connected with the Sorocabana but had its own station in the town, called the Estacão Paulo Souza. Paying a visit on October 1st 1978, I found to my pleasure locomotive No. 3 (GE 28558/1946) in the station, in a nice dark green livery. Passenger services, however, had already ceased.

I went on to the Votoran Cement Factory and found the younger electric No. 4 (GE 32389/1956), also in dark-green livery, shunting in front of the fence. But the plant had more to offer than just some one-off electrics, because the clouds could be seen and the hissing be heard of a steam locomotive working in the factory yard. Alas it was a Sunday and no manager was present who could have permitted access, and the guard at the entrance was firm in his refusal. Yet never give up: my hosts at São Paulo made a "connection" and I returned on October 4th for an official visit, and there was ex-Sorocabana 4-6-0 No. 415, wood-fired, in a light-blue colour scheme, built Lima 1289/1913, quite unusual as Lima was not a frequent exporter to South America. What remains to be said is that EFEV No. 1 (GE 28556/1946) was also there, loading freight cars with bagged cement, in a light-blue livery different from that of

EFEV no. 3, a General Electric 40-ton Bo-Bo in the Estacão Paulo Souza.

its sisters, and there was also a FEPASA diesel which worked the transfers. Was it a forecast of the future? According to Carter's book the EFEV was dieselised in 1986.

Rio de Janeiro is certainly one of the most beautiful cities of the world, but in terms of railways it was not an Eldorado, although two lovely little electric lines can still be found. The Santa Teresa Tramway or "Bonde" has its terminus near the Largo da Carioca in central Rio de Janeiro. On its climb to the old suburb of Santa Teresa it traverses the historic "Aqueduto", also called "Arcosi" (arches), seen in the adjacent photo with three of the tramway's "toast-rack" style streetcars.

Sta. Teresa Tramway. Tram cars on the Aqueduto ("Arcosi") in Rio de Janeiro, August 1974.

The other line is the rack railway up to the summit of Corcovado, which has an interesting history. It was built 1883 to the plans of Niklaus Riggenbach, former CME of the Swiss Central Railway at Olten. The length is 3.8 km, with a ruling grade of 30%. It was constructed to metre gauge, with a Riggenbach rack and used steam locomotives supplied by Olten Works, Baldwin, and Esslingen. The line was electrified in 1910 with 3-phase a.c. of 750 V / 50 Hz, using locomotives built by SLM (Winterthur). It was closed in 1969, but re-opened in 1971 with two train sets repaired. Reconstruction took place in 1975 with 3-phase a.c. of 900 V / 60 Hz and bogie railcars from SLM, normally operating as double units. The photo on the left, taken in August 1974 at the top station, still shows one of the old wooden-bodied train sets of 1910-20 vintage.

ARGENTINA

The few photographs of Argentinean electric locomotives which I have show some very small engines on a very short railway at a very remote location, i.e. Rio Turbio, better known to steam enthusiasts as the far end of the former Red Ferro Industrial Rio Turbio (RFIRT) in the extreme South of Patagonia. Both the RFIRT and the mine at Rio Turbio were operated by the State Coal Mining Board (Yacimientos Carboniferes Fiscales, YCF). Coal was hauled to the surface by an electric underground railway of the same gauge as the RFIRT (750 mm), but little is known of its origin. A mine locomotive exhibited in the small open-air museum at Rio Turbio carried a plaque saying it was "of Russian origin 1955-1975", which may be an indication that the railway was built in the mid-1950s with Soviet technology, but this needs to be confirmed. Reg Carter in his "Industrial Railways of Argentina" lists four locomotives built by AEC 1968 but has no details of others. The locomotives which I saw in December 1992, all of the four-wheel type, had no builder's plate or other identification. The coal was carried in 4-wheel cars of 4 tonnes capacity and discharged by tippler into a storage bunker, and workers were moved into and out of the mine in 4-wheel "passenger" cars.

December 1st 1992, was not a lucky day, as Rio Turbio had gone on strike and nothing, including the RFIRT, was working.

The rack railway to Corcovado peak on which stands the statue of Christ overlooking Rio de Janeiro. Coach no. 2 dating from 1910-20 leads as the train arrives at the top of the line.

YCF no. 20 with passenger coaches for the 750mm gauge mine railway at Rio Turbio.

Fortunately (for me), a few miners were still under ground and a workers train was made ready to rescue them, so I got at least one shot of a working locomotive, YCF 20, in "passenger service" (above), but none of a coal train. When I returned four years later Rio Turbio had been privatised and undergone "modernisation". The underground railway had been replaced by a conveyor belt, rails and catenary had been lifted and heaps of mine cars were piled up upside-down, but none of the electric locomotives were visible. The RFIRT was in the process of dieselisation and we possibly saw the last steam-hauled train on that tour. Recent reports say that mining at Rio Turbio has completely been closed down.

CHILE

The F.C. de Santiago a Valparaiso had been electrified as early as 1924 but electrification of the railway southwards from Santiago, known as the F.C. del Sur, did not start until the early 1960s, and was only completed to Temuco in 1987. Both of these railways were built to the 5'6" (1676 mm) gauge and electrified with 3000 V d.c., but while the Santiago-Valparaiso electrification was undertaken by Westinghouse, work on the Southern Railway was initiated by an Italian consortium Grupo Aziende Italiana, GAI), and later carried on by the Ferrocarriles del Estado themselves. Motive power for the F.C. del Sur comprises three types of electric locomotives, all supplied from Italy:

Class E-30, Bo-Bo, 2400 hp (1770 kW), 22 units built Ansaldo/Breda 1961.

Class E-32, Co-Co, 4500 hp (3310 kW), 24 units built Breda/Marelli 1961/62.

Class E-17, Bo-Bo, 1950 hp (1430 kW), 24 units built GAI 1973-75.

The two earlier classes had been built in that attractive long-nose streamline styling more typical of the forties and fifties while the E-17 had a prosaic centre-cab design. A visit to Santiago's San Eugenio depot on 30th November 1990 gave an opportunity to see examples of all three classes lying idle at home and the photo below presents two of them, E-1721 in front with long-nosed E-3015 behind it. The early morning photo of E-3201, which worked the night passenger to Temuco three days later, shows it at the local depot (opposite page, top right).

The northern Atacama desert still offers a most attractive electric industrial railway, the FC Tocopilla al Toco (FCTT). Built to the 3'6" (1067 mm) "Cape" gauge by the London-based Anglo-Chilean Nitrate & Railway Company, it served to connect the rich nitrate deposits on the Pampa del Toco with a deep water port on the Pacific Coast named Tocopilla. In 1925 the British company was bought out by the Guggenheim group of New York, which invested heavily in both the nitrate workings and the FCTT. One effect was the electrification, with 1500 V d.c., of the steep ascent from sea level up

Chilean broad gauge locomotives at San Eugenio on 30th November 1990. Nearest is E-1724 built by Breda in 1975 with E-3015 behind, constructed by Ansaldo in1961.

the coastal escarpment to Barriles (km 27.7 / elevation 1001 m), on a ruling grade of 4.1%, and onwards on lesser grades to El Tigre (km 39.2 / elev. 1296 m). Seven Bo-Bo locomotives were supplied by General Electric 1927/28 weighing 60 t, power 720 kW permanent / 878 kW one-hour, tractive force 96 kN permanent / 178 kN maximum. One of these, No. 601 (GE 10152/1927), is shown below right with a "visitors special" on 3rd November 1990 in that moon-like Atacama landscape short of Barriles.

A few words about the present situation. The nitrate industry had been nationalised In 1968 but was re-privatised in the mid-1980s and taken over by a consortium called the Sociedad Quimica y Minera (SQM). The FCTT, the plant railways of the Maria Elena and Pedro de Valdivia mining and processing plants, and the Tocopilla port facilities were transferred to a daughter company called Servicios Integrales de Transitos y Transferencias (SIT). In 1997 the locomotives were lettered "SIT" and some already carried a new blue and white colour scheme, while others, among them no. 601 shown below, still had the original orange livery.

When I saw the FCTT again in 2001 the locos were lettered "SQM" and the colour scheme had again been altered into bright green and blue, but one (No. 603) still had the old FCTT orange. No. 605 has been scrapped but the others were still kept in working order, although they were suffering from age and lack of spares, understandably. As a relief the current has been turned off on the Barriles - El Tigre section which is diesel worked, but the railway's CME said they had not so far found any suitable replacement for the electrics on the heavily graded ascent to Barriles.

BOLIVIA

Bolivia had only a short section of public electrified railway, i.e. the 9 km ascent from La Paz to El Alto of the metre-gauge F.C. Guaqui (FCG). Its history and motive power were described by Ian Thomson in Locomotives International issue no. 9 and need not be duplicated here. Remarkably this section, built on grades of up to an unbelievable 7%, was electric-operated with 550 V d.c. almost from the start, i.e. from 1908,

E-3201, seen at Temuco on 3rd December 1990, represents the FC del Sur's other Italian-built class, this loco being the class leader supplied by Breda in 1961.

and was indeed the first electric railway in all South America.

The largest, and last, of its electric locomotives was Bo-Bo No. 32 (English Electric 768/1930), which was still working on shunting duties when seen at La Paz on 24th October 1978 (overleaf). But the FCG line to El Alto was already closed and Guaqui trains were diesel-hauled over the easier ex-FCAB route. Today, this has also been disposed of, and rails no longer reach down into La Paz.

SIT / FCTT 'boxcab' No. 601 on the Tocopill-Barriles section of the FCTT with an assortment of ancient carriages.

41

Bo-Bo-Bo hood type locomotives numbered BBB-50 to 55 were received from Alsthom. The overhead transmission system uses a.c. of 25 kV / 60 Hz while the traction motors work on 2000 V d.c., conversion being made by a rotary motor-generator on board the locomotive. The railway was interesting for steam enthusiasts as a couple of steam locomotives were still active on shunting and trip work while the main line was the domain of the electrics. I saw one of them depart from Paz del Rio with a train of empties but too late to get a shot, and of course the steamers had priority, so the train went away unchased. Two engines lay idle in the yard and BBB-50 was photographed on 22nd August 1988. Two more were seen under repair in the workshop.

FC Guaqui's English Electric Bo-Bo no. 32 shunting at La Paz, Bolivia, in October 1978.

COLOMBIA

Electric railways in Colombia? Yes, there is one, the industrial railway of the Acerias Paz del Rio steelworks near Sogamoso, some 250 km north-east of Bogota on the former F.C. del Nordeste. The steel plant, which was constructed in 1953, consumes iron ore and coal from deposits lying close together about 30 km away. Also in 1953 the F.C. del Nordeste, originally of metre gauge, was re-gauged to 3 ft (914 mm) in order to conform with the other railways in the country, and at the same time was extended by 6 km from Sogamoso to Paz del Rio. As a consequence the industrial railway which links the steel plant to its mines was also built to that gauge. Its main line was subsequently electrified, in this case with French technology, and six

REFERENCES

R. Carter, Railways of Brazil, published by the author 2002.
W. Hefti, Zahnradbahnen der Welt, 2 Vols.,
    Birkhäuser, Basel 1971/1976.
R. Carter, Industrial Railways of Argentina,
    published by the author 1998.
W.F. Simms, The Railways of Chile Vols. 3 & 4,
    published by the author 2000/2001.
D. Binns, The Anglo-Chilean Nitrate and Railway Company,
    Trackside Publications 1996.
I. Thomson, Locomotives International no. 9 (1991) p. 2.
P.A. Catchpole, A Very British Railway,
    Locomotives International, St. Teath, 2003.

Three foot gauge Acerias Paz del Rio Bo-Bo-Bo no. BBB-50, built by Alsthom circa 1960 and pictured in Colombia in August 1988.

Some Aspects of Romanian Diesel Traction, Some Early Projects

by Gottfried Wild

To those people who visited Eastern Europe and had the opportunity to visit Romania, especially in the 1955 - 1980 period, that country surely left a fingerprint of particular originality in their minds. This originality concerns both the people itself and its culture, its gastronomy and last but not least, the railway transport. On this subject, the period features an extremely varied jigsaw puzzle of locomotives and rolling stock, such that one could sometimes think every train was pulled by its own and individual and never replicated locomotive! Watching a train in a station in the late 1950s the knowledgeable railway observer could also think that a complete technological era was rolling along the rails, because it included almost everything created for railways during the last five decades… Standardisation seemed to be an unknown word there and steam was everywhere on the metals. Steam, steam wherever you look and once again, steam!

Due to its rich oil sources Romania was able to support a large fleet of steam locomotives with quite a unique aspect created in that country: the locomotives were fired both with coal and with oil. Romania also features some very steep gradients with double heading and bankers being a daily sight on almost every train in those steamy days. The additional oil firing was of great help to the firemen, considerably relieving them from hard work. Some enthusiasts may ask today, if so, why did they ever introduce diesel and electric traction?

The greatest challenge for locomotive constructors and also for footplate staff, was the (Bucharest) - Câmpina - Brasov main line, culminating in grades of 1 in 48 to 1 in 50 at the summit of the line at Predeal, fig. 1. Quite regularly, four or even five engines were recorded pulling and pushing heavy freight trains across the Carpathian Mountains from Bucharest to Transylvania. Imagine this dramatic spectacle in winter time under terrible blizzard conditions, along the deep Carpathian valleys, up into the mountains… Winter is generally frightening in Romania! Certainly, an impressive scene, especially when amalgamated with steam traction.

While enthusiasts or even laymen were admiring such regular

exciting technical events, higher officers of the Romanian railway administration, CFR, had recognised many years earlier how uneconomical such a kind of an operation was, in spite of rich oil resources. No wonder activities relating to the subject of dieselisation had been discussed in Romania soon after the end of WW1, electrification even earlier.

Internal combustion on Romanian rails had first appeared as early as 1907 when a pair of petrol-electric four wheeled 70 hp railcars were introduced. They were manufactured at the works of Johann Weitzer at Arad, Transylvania. Just one year earlier, in Transylvania again, the Austro-Hungarian railway administration had introduced petrol-engined railcars on the Arad - Cenad/Csanady section. Between 1923 and 1930, Prof. Bákonyi Kolomàn, the former CME of the Arad - Cenad branch line, then employed by the CFR, had presented several official papers to the railway administration supporting the introduction of internal combustion engines for branch-line operation. This kind of railway operation, diesel traction and light vehicles, found extremely advantageous conditions in Romania.

For many years there it was common practice to run mixed trains including both freight and passenger cars on branch lines, which was perhaps relatively economical with regard to locomotive usage but the scheduled running times included shunting goods wagons at almost every station! To avoid this inconvenience dating back to the stone-age of railway operation, it was intended to give up mixed trains, the passenger duties being transferred to light railcars with, naturally, higher operational speeds and lower costs. Romania had at that time a large and dense network of railways while road transport was still undeveloped. We understand now why the country offered the best conditions for railcar introduction and development.

The Astra Works of Arad in Western Transylvania were already involved in railcar manufacturing, their technology influenced by the Hungarian experience and progress in this domain. In 1933 a new competitor appeared on the Romanian railcar market: the Malaxa Works of Bucharest, founded by Nicolae

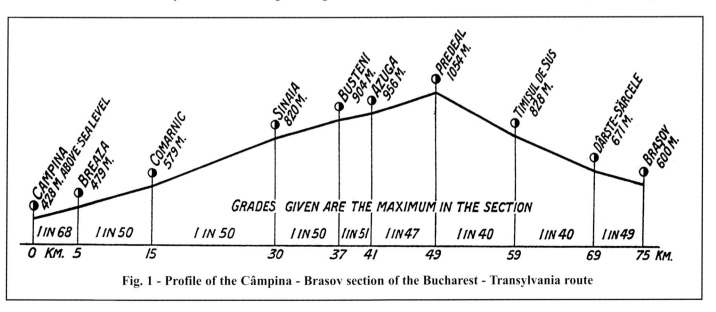

Fig. 1 - Profile of the Câmpina - Brasov section of the Bucharest - Transylvania route

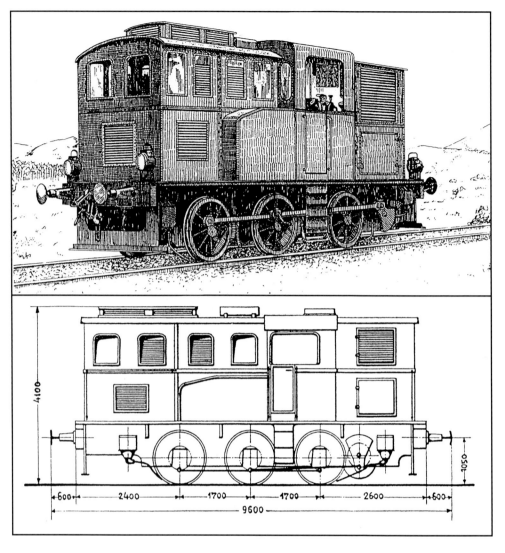

Figs 2 & 3. Diagram (1:87 scale) and artist's impression of a Romanian 0-6-0 diesel locomotive with hydraulic drive for shunting service.

didn't own any of the required facilities, not even a workshop hall! But just 12 months later the first heavy steam locomotive emerged from a new erecting shop according to the contract he had signed.

The same energy was applied to his experiments with railcars. Recalling similar Biblical tales about seven years of plagues, Nicolae Malaxa spent seven unsuccessful years on different experiments searching for reliable technical solutions for this kind of railway vehicle and also spending enormous sums of money. It was said in those days that the money he earned from steam locomotive construction was all wasted on railcar experiments! Obviously, Malaxa was fascinated by the internal combustion engine and was looking ahead to a promising future with this form of traction.

But in 1937 Malaxa, who meanwhile was testing large eight-wheeled bogie railcar prototypes, was able to present the results of his remarkable and we can say, heroic efforts at the Belgrade Technical Fair. There, his fine looking railcars were admired alongside the most modern products from traditional and long-established manufacturers like Fiat and Ganz. In 1940, at another Technical Fair at Milan, Italy, Malaxa introduced a high-speed streamlined bogie railcar and an 0-4-0 rod-driven diesel-

Malaxa, an extremely dynamic and forward-looking engineer and entrepreneur. Malaxa entered the steam locomotive business at the beginning of 1928 then in 1933 he started experiments with railcars. The first prototypes were rebuilt from older four-wheeled passenger cars, equipped with an internal combustion engine and gears. In the beginning, Malaxa used the Constantinescu gear. George Constantinescu was an 1881-born Romanian engineer and inventor who had established himself in 1912 in Great Britain. In 1931 Constantinescu heeded Malaxa's call and returned to Bucharest together with two British technicians. On the long journey from England these gentlemen had to carry some very large luggage indeed as they brought a range of nine different engines of British design to be presented to the Romanian officials.

Nicolae Malaxa was educated as a mechanical engineer at the Karlsruhe University of Baden in Germany and soon proved to possess very practical intuition when "attacking" technical problems. His methods were simple and adventurous, sometimes even risky. As a young engineer and owner of a wooden building which he considered as a factory, Malaxa didn't hesitate to start locomotive and rolling stock repairs under the hot and sunny, or rainy, and sometimes even frosty sky! He signed a contract for the production of 0-10-0 freight locomotives at a moment when he

mechanical shunting locomotive, together with the impressive prototype of an entirely Romanian-developed heavy 2-10-2 steam locomotive. We note, he had made the first step towards diesel locomotive construction too. Just a few months later this promising evolution was interrupted by the outbreak of World War 2. In spite of all difficulties, Malaxa continued to supply heavy steam locomotives to the CFR together with 13 further units of an articulated bogie high-speed railcar type until 1944. By then Romania had entered the international family of countries able to run railcars self-manufactured at quite an elevated technological level.

If Malaxa was the youngest locomotive manufacturer in Romania, there were others in that country producing locomotives and rolling stock too. The Resita Works in Transylvania was an old and traditional metallurgical manufacturer, dating back to Habsburg imperial times. At the time when Nicolae Malaxa had established his own works in Bucharest, locomotive construction was already a historical fact in the city of Resita. No wonder, as they were competitive on the international locomotive market, offering some interesting locomotive proposals for railway administrations in Turkey, Egypt, Greece and even Argentina, at the same time supplying locomotives for the indigenous main line, and for shunting and industrial purposes. The history of the

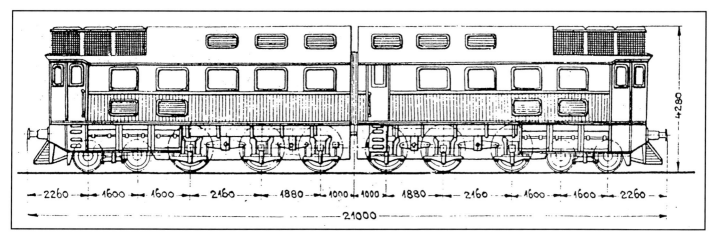

Fig. 4 & 5 - Diagram (1:120 scale) and artist's impression of a heavy Romanian 2Co+Co2 articulated diesel locomotive with electric drive for main line services.

Resita Works has already been described in the columns of the Locomotives International; further information may be extracted from the titles mentioned in the sources too.

Having learned about the problems confronting Romanian diesel traction as well as the industrial and technological development of the country, let's have a look at the drawing boards now. We have already mentioned railcars, but locomotive projects will also be discussed. In particular the previously mentioned heavy gradients on the Câmpina - Predeal - Brasov main line were a subject for several studies and projects with alternative traction systems. Electrification of this route was discussed in 1913, but was interrupted by a World conflagration within a year. Electrification studies continued during the 1920s and 1930s, and the Germans were closely supporting Romania with a first practical step in this direction during the 1940s, however, catenary for regular use would not be switched on until as late as 1966…

The 1928 Resita catalogue presents, among several exciting steam locomotive projects, two standard gauge diesel locomotives. One of them is a 40 ton 0-6-0 centre-cab locomotive for shunting services, figs. 2 + 3. It would have been, if materialised, a rod driven prototype using a four-stroke diesel at a maximum output of 360 hp. Power transmission to the jackshaft placed at one end of the locomotive was by a Lentz hydraulic gear. Although the locomotive was intended for shunting, its maximum speed at 50 km/h indicates intentions for occasional use on light branch line freight services.

The next design is more impressive, featuring a heavy articulated 2Co+Co2 diesel-electric main line locomotive, figs. 4 & 5. At the end of the 1920s traffic over the Predeal Pass was operated with 0-10-0 and 2-8-0 locomotives of German pattern in concert with "Pershing" Consolidations from Baldwin and it is supposed that the Resita diesel would replace steam traction on this route.

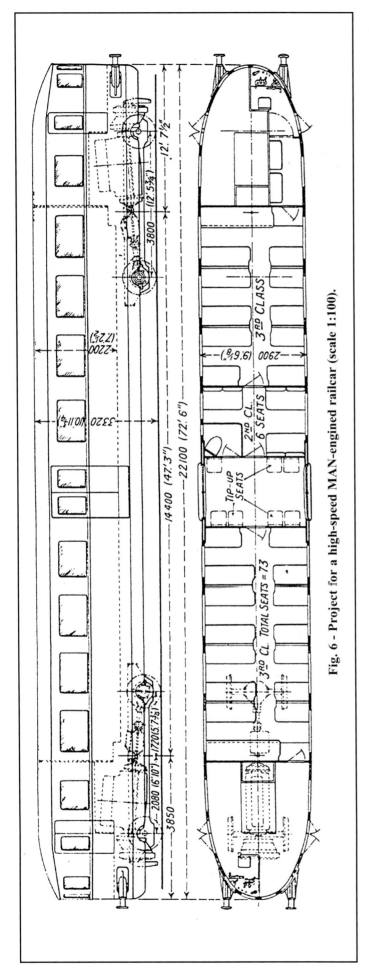

Fig. 6 - Project for a high-speed MAN-engined railcar (scale 1:100).

This project featured an 8-cylinder four-stroke engine per unit, being able to supply an output of 1035 hp at the maximum engine speed of 580 rpm. A train heating device, using exhaust gases from the engines during winter suggests that the locomotive was intended for passenger service too, in spite of its relatively low maximum running speed, limited to 75 km/h. At 55 km/h the locomotive would have an indicated power of 1800 hp. During summer time, the thermal energy intended for the train heating system would have activated a multiple cascade air ejector for the cooling circuit of the engines, based upon a Resita patent. The radiators were placed at the front ends of the locomotive cabs, on the roof, and the attentive reader may have noticed indeed that the locomotive lacks the typical ventilation fans. Unfortunately the project never came to fruition so the question of how reliable the Resita technology for diesel traction could really have been, remains a mystery.

Almost ten years later in 1938, a large prototype of a 4400 hp diesel locomotive, interestingly an articulated design again, entered service on the Predeal division. At that time this locomotive was the most powerful diesel in Europe. This fine looking 2Do1+1Do2 locomotive with electric drive, which emerged from the firm of Sulzer in Switzerland, should have stood at the head of a large fleet of similar locomotives in, however, at the end of the 1930s the political and economic situation in Europe was not favourable to such projects. The "Sulzer", as this locomotive is still known in Romania, remained a single apparition, but she was fortunately saved and superbly restored, though not to working order. Sulzer was to have a new entry on Romanian rails in 1959 with its excellent (and actually still working) Class 060 DA Co-Co diesel-electrics, but that is another story.

Contrary to Malaxa, Resita's manufacturing was profiled only upon heavy industrial products such as locomotives so, according to available sources, we will not find any railcar projects emerging its drawing office. At the same time a continuously increasing fleet of four or eight-wheeled railcars using alternatively MAN, Ganz or Deutz engines in conjunction with Mylius, TAG or Ganz mechanical drives were supplied both by the Malaxa and the Astra Works. The Diesel Railway Traction Gazette of 1938 records that the previous year 192 diesel and petrol railcars were in regular use on main and branch-line duties in Romania.

The June 1935 issue of this British railway magazine published an interesting project for a high-speed streamlined railcar for the Romanian State Railways, fig. 6. It was to be fitted with two light 150 hp MAN engines driving the inner axle of each bogie through Mylius mechanical gears. The vehicles were intended for single operation at 80 mph. The project continues to be a kind of a mystery, reaching up into the present day because the magazine states 'the Romanian State Railways has ordered a number of double-ended diesel railcars shown in the accompanying diagram'. If any kind of practical activity had ever really been started on this project, information is completely lacking.

Romanian studies and activities centred upon diesel traction were continuously pursued, as contemporary literature proves. Ion Cudalbu, a noted personality in the contemporary Romanian dieselisation studies, offers an interesting study regarding the future of diesel railcar operation in Romania. His projects will be discussed in the following paragraphs.

A non-dated project, presumably from the beginning of the 1940s, features an interesting lightweight three unit railcar set,

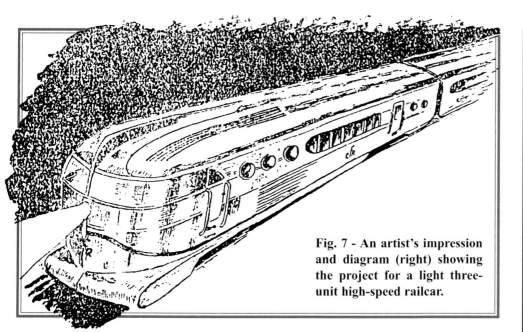

Fig. 7 - An artist's impression and diagram (right) showing the project for a light three-unit high-speed railcar.

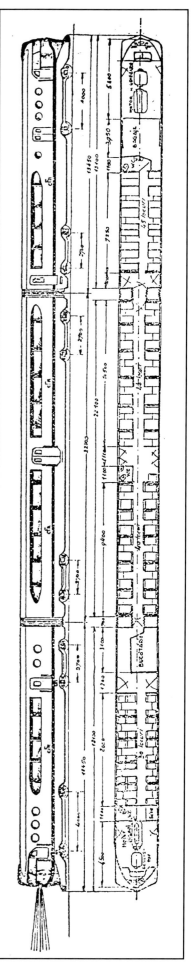

fig. 7. It is indeed, a very futuristic view of a railway vehicle, but it suits contemporary fashion precisely, with American characteristics. This railcar set would be motorised at either end by a diesel electric power plant rated at 650 hp. Speed was limited to 140 km/h, the railcar having a kitchen in one of the motorised cars. No indications are made of a restaurant section so it is presumed that meals would have been offered to the passengers at their seats in the modern aeroplane manner. The total number of seats was configured at 160, total weight of the train in working order at 169 tons. Air conditioned and supplementary electro-magnetic brakes were other features of this vehicle. Certainly, it was intended for operation on superior comfort services.

The next project for a Romanian railcar was intended for long-distance main line journeys. Amazingly, this quite heavy four-unit set is an original amalgamation of American and German characteristics! Fig. 8. While the outline is doubtless inspired from contemporary US diesel locomotives, with possible further design inspirations from the 20th Century Limited, the technical characteristics indicate German sources. Two very similar four-unit long-distance prototypes were introduced by the Reichsbahn administration in 1938 as Class SVT 137 Berlin, running numbers 901-903. As with the German model, the Romanians intended to place a diesel-electric aggregate at one end of the train, designing in this case a separate power unit or, a light-weight Bo-Bo locomotive. The very American looking Romanian railcar would run on Görlitz bogies and the central automatic couplings at both ends were of Scharfenberg design. Maximum speed was limited again at 140 km/h due to a 1200 hp motor. Total number of seats was 270, and weight in working order was estimated at 257.4 tons. Again, air-conditioning and additional electromagnetic brakes would be fitted. The non-powered end car was a restaurant with 40 seats, the streamlined portion forming an observation compartment. Luxury, par excellence!

Branch line operation would not have been neglected in Ion Cudalbu´s studies for the CFR either. For this purpose, a light diesel-mechanical railcar running on bogies was proposed, capable of operation in multiple units. A 220 hp diesel aggregate would allow a maximum speed of 100 km/h. Total weight in working order, 42 tons. The streamlined outline looks quite American again, fig. 9. The floor plan of the vehicle indicates a small buffet area as well as a further luggage compartment.

None of these projects described ever came into practice, unfortunately. For both unknown and for very realistic reasons, such as the outbreak and repercussions of WW2, these designs never left the drawing board. Nevertheless the studies and the creative energy spent around them were in the end a valuable support in enabling the realisation of other designs. They also describe the way in which dieselisation was perpetuated in Romania in the end, allowing in these columns an insight into a country sometimes little known to the western European citizen.

Finally, in spite of war, destruction, and dictatorship, Romania continued its railcar tradition, with some "ups" and "downs" through the decades, into the present. Last but not least,

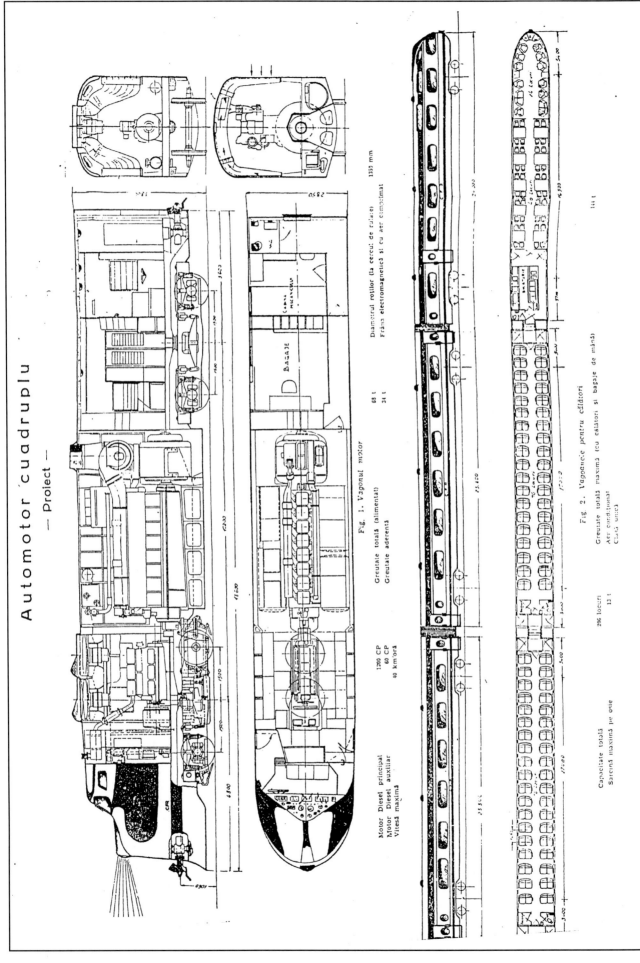

Automotor cuadruplu
— Proiect —

Motor Diesel principal   1200 CP
Motor Diesel auxiliar   60 CP
Viteză maximă   40 km/oră

Fig. 1. *Vagonul motor*

Greutate totală (alimentat)   68 t
Greutate aderentă   34 t

Diametrul roţilor (la cercul de rulare)   1350 mm
Frâna electromagnetică şi cu aer comprimat

Fig. 2. *Vagonul pentru călători*

Capacitate totală   296 locuri
Sarcină maximă pe osie   13 t

Greutate totală maximă (cu călători şi bagaje de mână)   14 t
Aer condiţionat
Clasă unică

Fig. 8 – Project for a heavy four-unit high-speed railcar.

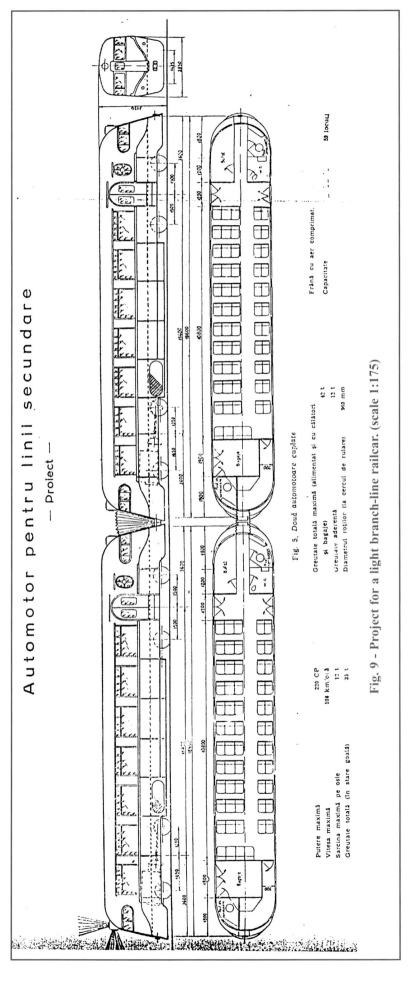

Automotor pentru linii secundare
— Proiect —

Fig. 5. Două automotoare cuplate

Greutate totală maximă (alimentat şi cu călători)   42 t
  şi bagaje)   12 t
Greutate aderentă   12 t
Diametrul rotilor (la cercul de rulare)   940 mm

Frână cu aer comprimat.
Capacitate   59 locuri

Putere maximă   220 CP
Viteza maximă   104 km/oră
Sarcina maximă pe osie   12 t
Greutate totală (în stare goală)   35 t

Fig. 9 – Project for a light branch-line railcar. (scale 1:175)

those early projects and studies speak for quality and, together with practical work done in the factories behind the Carpathians, allow us 60 years later in the present day, to admire some of the old Malaxa or Astra-built railcars at work. In Europe, Romania is a railway oasis indeed, where such historical vehicles are still on the rails. Some of them, refurbished and re-engined, are continuously doing good passenger service on several branch lines of that country. Little has changed over the last 60 years in Romania, or has it? Try to find out for yourself, as it is worth seeing those old vehicles at work!

Sources:

Locomotive si cazane.   U.D.R. Resita, 1928

Automotoarele la Caile Ferate Romane.
  Ing. A. Zanescu, Ing. A. Derevici. Bucharest, 1937

Les Autorails des Chemins de fer Roumains,
  Ing. Aurel Zanescu.
  Traction Nouvelle, no. 14, Paris, 1938

Diesel Railway Traction, June 1935.
  Fast Diesels for Romania

Diesel Railway Traction, January 1938.
  Railcar Practice in Romania

Diesel Railway Traction, February 1938.
  Fast twin-car Trains in Romania

Diesel Railway Traction, October 1938.
  Romanian Main Line Locomotive Performance

The Locomotive, June 1938.
  High-power Diesel Locomotive for Romania

Die Lokomotive, August 1941.
  4400 PS dieselelektrische Schnellzug-
  Lokomotive für die Rumänische Eisenbahn

Motortechnische Zeitschrift, 1942.
  Dieselelektrische 4400 PS-Lokomotive
  der Rumänischen Staatsbahn

Analele CFR.   Consideratiuni asupra problemei
  automotoarelor la CFR. Ing. Ion Cudalbu, Bucharest

The Locomotives of Romania,
  C J Halliwell, Frank Stenvall, Malmö, 1970

Uzinele Malaxa,   Dr. Ing. Henry Holban.
  Magazin Istoric, Bucharest, 1991

LOKi, 6/7/8-1994, Fachpresse Goldach AG, Zürich.
  Schweizer Qualität: Sulzer-Diesellok von 1938

Istoria locomotivelor si a cailor ferate din Banatul Montan,
  Ing. Dan Perianu. Editura Timpul, Resita, 2000

Diesel Locomotives of the Wangerooge Island Railway *by Wolfgang Ewers*

This feature supplements a full article about the railway on Wangerooge island published in the L.I. special edition "Steam & Rail in Germany"

In 1996/97 the three 1,000 mm gauge Gmeinder diesels acquired by DB in the 1950s were still hauling most of the trains on the island. These three-axle diesels, then numbered 399.101 to 399.103 were used almost exclusively in passenger service between the Western pier and the village. The four-axle Deutz diesel was chiefly employed for shunting. As the two Romanian-built diesels proved to be rather unreliable in service they were only seldom used.

With the three "original" diesels being in constant use for 40 years or more DB AG decided to replace the ageing engines with new ones built by Christoph Schoettler Maschinenbau GmbH (Schoema) of Diepholz. In April 1999 two four-wheel diesel-hydraulics (model CFL-150 DCL) which were almost identical with those previously built for the 900 mm gauge Borkum island railway arrived on the island. Numbered 399.107 and 399.108 they soon took over the duties of the Gmeinder diesels.

By this date 399.101 had already been set aside following an engine failure in 1998. Sister engine 399.103 was withdrawn in Winter 1999/2000 and the last of the trio, 399.102, was working its last train in Summer 2000. At the same time 399.104 ("Heinrich") was put into store.

Only in May 2001 were all four locomotives officially removed from the inventory. Exactly a year later all of them were sold to the "Foerderverein der Rügenschen Kleinbahnen e V." (Supporters of the Rügen Island Light Railways). As the light railways on the island of Rügen in the Baltic Sea have been built to a gauge of 750 mm, the ex-Wangerooge locomotives will have to be rebuilt before going into service.

The two Romanian diesels remained on the island: 399.106 has been given another thorough overhaul and now works satisfactorily. 399.105 serves as a spare engine and is only used sporadically now.

Not the bridge of the ferry boat but the footplate of 399.101. The 'steering wheel' is actually the power handle!

Maid of all work, diesel hydraulic no. 399.102 propels a loaded freight train carrying containers of different sizes into the head shunt of Wangerooge station, 24th September 1996.

399.104 was named 'Heinrich' when running on the Juist Island Railway, from where it was leased in 1971 to cover a shortage of engines on the Wangerooge system and bought by DB a year later. It was the only four-wheel locomotive on Wangerooge and was used almost exclusively for shunting until stored in the summer of 2000.

399.103, on the right inside the shed, was built by Messrs. Gmeinder at Mosbach in 1957 and was always known as a reliable performer. The same could not be said of nos. 399.105 and 399.106 (built in Bucharest in 1990) which when seen here on 24th September 1996 were already stored unserviceable.

Romanian built diesel-hydraulic no. 399.106 was out of use due to failure of the electrical system and waiting at the back of Wangerooge shed in September 1996 for spares to arrive. Sister engine 399.105 was in a similar state. In due course complete overhauls turned these two former Mansfeld Transport locomotives into useable machines.

In 1914 London Motor Omnibus Company (England) took delivery of some AEC/Daimler type 506 buses equipped with 45hp petrol engines. They were sufficiently successful for the chassis to be used for lorries and adapted for rail vehicles.

In the 1920s the 3'6" gauge Queensland Railways needed new railmotors to replace an older fleet of vehicles and decided to import the AEC chassis to adapt as the basis of a new design. Conversion of the chassis to rail use and construction of the metal-sided bodywork was undertaken at Ipswich workshops, Queensland, the first example being rolled out on 21st April 1927. Seven more were built that year and seven more each in 1928 and 1929, plus another ten in 1930 and five in 1931. One of their strangest features of the railmotors was a plate on the engine bulkhead stating that they were not be used within 15 miles of Charing Cross! The reason for this was that the London bus company had the sole right to use the type 506 within this area and the plates were fitted to all new chassis manufactured.

The front wheels were replaced by a bogie and 3' diameter flanged wheels were fitted at the back. The coachwork was built unglazed at the sides due to the warm climate in the summer and with pull-down blinds for shade against the sun and for protection against wind and rain at other times of the year. Accommodation was on benches fitted across the body in six compartments, including the driver's, each with a door either side. Three passengers could sit beside the driver, who also had room for tools under the bench and a space for tools and

This impossible animal is a railmotor! So declared my Aunt on the back of this photo. It was taken around 1950 on a visit to Queensland after she had emigrated as a 'ten-pound Pom'. A trip north took in Townsville, where this particular car, RM54 was based around that time. Photo: Patricia Farley.

a first aid box in the roof extension over the windscreen. Total passenger capacity was for 28 people seated. Five of the railmotors intended for lines where they would provide the sole motive power were constructed with the doors in pairs to enable larger items to be loaded. These were nos. 23-25 (Etheridge), 31 (Normanton) and 32 (Cooktown) - numberings as after 1929, as explained further on.

The driving controls were mainly as in the road bus but with the throttle as a hand-operated lever - and of course no steering wheel! Extra controls were fitted for sanding equipment and air brakes, both acting on the rear wheels. The hand-brake acted on the front bogie wheels, the motion and effort for both braking systems being transmitted through rods and levers. Evidently engine control systems were not what we understand today (or even as they were in the author's old Morris Traveller) as a small lever had to be provided for the driver to advance the spark ignition when engine speed rose. Electrical power for the engine and lights came from a magneto, while the compressor for air braking was driven off the engine's fan belt. There was no battery, so to start the engine the driver turned a permanently mounted crank handle. Younger readers accustomed to

RM60 at Normanton on 4th February 1991. This had been the last railmotor in use and is now preserved.   *Photo: Stan Berry.*

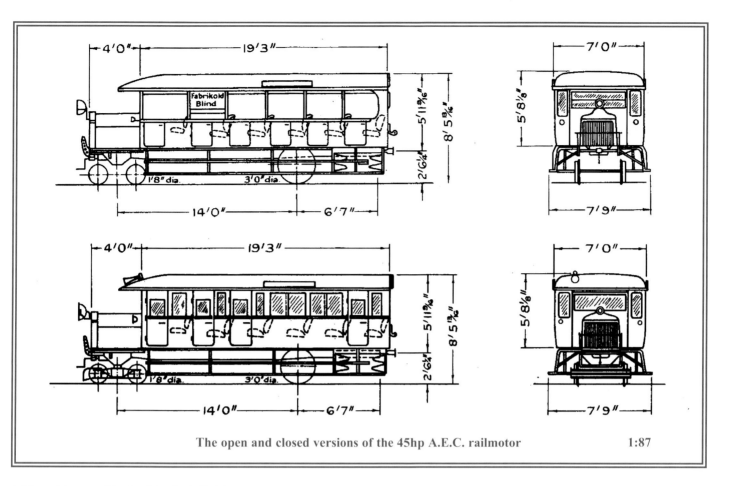

The open and closed versions of the 45hp A.E.C. railmotor   1:87

'chips with everything' might find all this somewhat bizarre!

Each railmotor was also provided with two trailers, one with seats for 30 passengers and another for carrying goods. The passenger trailers were built with similar bodywork to the railmotor and were carried on three axles. Later some larger bogie passenger trailers were built with a 50 seat capacity, the unladen weight of the two types being 3¼ and 6½ tons respectively. With the railmotors weighing about 6 tons this made for a 108-seater train of less than 15 tons and a gross weight of only around 23 tons - less than a small locomotive alone.

The trailers were braked, both individually and by means of two air pressure braking systems linked to the driving car's compressor. Pipes from the air compressor led directly to the trailer brake cylinders and also fed a reservoir tank. In the event of the train splitting the guard in the trailer had an emergency tap which could be opened release air to the brake cylinders and stop the train. In addition, the bogie trailers had a screw brake inside the car and the six-wheelers had a lever on the outside. Coupling was by means of a bar attached by pins to the central buffer, backed up by a chain either side. Communication with the driver was by pulling on a leather strap linked to a bell above him on the ceiling.

The railmotors built up to 1929 were numbered RM34-39, RM57-62 and RM77-87, renumbered in that year (in sequence) to RM17-39. Subsequent railmotors were numbered RM42-45, RM50-52 and RM54-61.

Apart from replacing older railmotors, the success of the new vehicles led to many new services being set up. Mostly the railmotors were based on particular branch lines and performed a local link between towns and rural communities, particularly vital

in some areas without roads. They were operated pretty much as what they were - buses on rails. New stops were placed for them at locations such as level crossings, farms etc. Traffic apart from passengers included parcels, mail, cream and livestock, all transported at a modest pace as the maximum permitted speed was 30 miles per hour (just under 50 km/h). On the Cooktown and Normanton lines the Railmotors formed the entire railway service.

Modifications

The south of their operating range had a less favourable climate in winter so a dozen of the railmotors were given glazed windows in the period 1932 to 1935. The reconstruction involved was quite drastic as the sides were completely replaced using galvanised iron sheeting up to window level and timber and glass above. At the time of reconstruction provision was made for carrying water bags and a wire mesh was fitted to the window behind the driver to protect it from breakage during exchange of tokens. Doors with wind-down windows were placed on the left and right side of bench one (the driver's), on the left side of benches 2 and 3 and on the right side of benches 5 and 6. A narrow gap for people to pass through was made by a 1'3" shortening of the right-hand end of benches 1 to 3 and the left-hand end of benches 4 and 5. Passenger capacity was reduced by 4 people but the modifications were considered a great improvement. The cars concerned were nos. 17, 22, 26, 28, 30, 33, 36, 37, 45, 51, 55 and 61.

The same twelve railmotors received 50hp diesel engines from 1937 onwards, owing to the Melbourne and Metropolitan

Tramways Board having surplus Gardner Model 4LW motors available, to which were added a few more purchased new. Along with the diesel engines, batteries were fitted (has the reader ever tried cranking over a diesel engine by hand?) and the air compressor was moved so that it could be driven off the engine tailshaft.

RM22 was temporarily fitted to burn kerosene in 1933 and, along with RM26 received a roof rack for excess goods. In the case of RM22's Cooyar workings this was often used for carrying ice cream. RM38 was given a novel conversion in 1935 when the bodywork behind the driver's bench was replaced by a gauze mesh to convert it for carrying rabbits. It only lasted till 1941 though, when the car was withdrawn.

Withdrawals

When they were built the 45hp railmotors were expected to last 30 years, but the petrol engines only about 10 years. In fact by rebuilding the engines and perhaps using the ones taken out of the dieselised or prematurely withdrawn cars they were made to last as long as the rest of the vehicle. The vehicles were also kept as long as possible due to lack of funds for replacement and because they were economical and reliable. The mechanics and electrics were simple enough for emergency repairs to be sorted out by the drivers in the event of a problem out on the line.

Withdrawal dates are thus:

1941	RM38 (rabbit car)
1945	RM31
1947	RM18
1951	RM27
1953	RM29
1954	RM24/35/52
1956	RM42/57
1958	RM21 (after an accident)
1959	RM23/25
1960	RM32/43/56
1961	RM34/44/58/59
1962	RM19/20/36/39/45/50/54
1962-3*	RM17/22/26/30
1963-4*	RM28/37/51/60/61
1964-5*	RM33
1966	RM55

* financial year

Cooktown's RM32 was named "Endeavour" and worked that line from 1929-44, when it was transferred to Normanton and worked there till January 1960. After withdrawal the engine and gearbox and other parts were removed for spares and in 1964 the vehicle went to Haydon as accommodation for track gangs. Unfortunately a collision occurred in 1977 and the body was burnt. The remains were preserved on the concrete base of the old toilets at Normanton in 1985 but eventually fell apart.

RM34/44/58 were sold with the Cooktown Railway for scrap. RM60 at Normanton was the last of the petrol-engined cars in use. In 1960 all of the diesel-engined railmotors were still in service and RM55 at Townsville was used in that year to deputise for the prestige air-conditioned 'Sunlander'. The line north of Ayr was too heavily flooded for the luxury train to pass but the railmotors were allowed to run through floodwater up to a foot deep, so RM55 was brought south with two trailers as a temporary replacement. RM28 was purchased for excursion service by the Aramac Shire Council, while RM60 remained at Normanton and is now preserved. RM55 also still exists, having been used by the Australian Railway Historical Society between Ipswich and Grandchester until August 1966 and thereafter set aside.

More modern railmotors

In 1930 Queensland Railways turned an AEC 100hp bus chassis into a railmotor, RM40, the first enclosed railcar since the five McKeen cars (featured in Diesels and Electrics special edition no. 1). In 1931 two other chassis were turned out with the older 45hp engine (RM62/63) and another 100hp variant (RM53). In the same year some much larger railcars were produced powered by Leyland 100hp engines (RM46/47) and 150hp Winton engines (RM48/49). The best features of the foregoing were then combined in a type built on the AEC 100hp chassis with the enclosed sides of RM62/63 and the greater internal headroom of RM46-49. Other improvements included roller bearings on the front bogie, a 40 mph top speed and a toilet. Sixteen of these larger cars were built, numbers RM65 to RM80, each provided with two trailers, one of which had a luggage compartment taking up half the car. For the Etheridge Railway RM67 was built with the rear half of the railmotor as a goods compartment and RM74 was built with the rear half as a low-sided open truck.

Two AEC 100hp chassis were built with 102hp Gardner diesel engines in 1936, RM81/82. The front of these vehicles was

The wreck of the 'Endeavour' is all that remained of RM32 at Normanton in 1991. Photo: Stan Berry.

The Railmotor in use on the Normanton-Croydon line in 1998 and operating the "Gulflander" was one of the "streamliners", RM93, seen here at Blackbull with trailer 1811 on the 08:30 weekly service from Normanton.   Photo: Stan Berry.

enclosed with the sides sloping in to the radiator and the whole front sloping up to the roof, giving a more contemporary appearance for the time. Two more followed but with a fluid torque converter drive in place of the normal gearbox, RM83/84, but the 70hp output of the torque converter was a weakness as it did not permit the full power of the engine to be applied.

From 1937-1940 eight further examples were constructed with a longer body (33'3") which, having a rounded front, became known as the 'Streamliners', numbers RM85 to RM92. Two more under construction in 1940 were delayed by the war, not finally appearing until 1951, nos. RM93/94. These were the last of the railmotors based on the 1914 AEC/Daimler bus chassis and its developments, subsequent vehicles being of more conventional railcar construction.

For completeness though, mention should be made of two inspection cars of 4-2-0 wheel arrangement. RM16 of 1934 converted from an International road car and retaining the steering wheel - used to operate the brakes. The other car, RM64 of 1938, was based on a chassis roughly similar in design principles to the AEC railmotors, fitted with a Ford V-8 39hp engine and bodywork in the style of the "Streamliners".

Acknowledgements

Much of the information in this article has been extracted from the writings of J.W. Knowles, to whom all credit is due for the original research. Mr. Knowles wrote and published in Brisbane "Lonely Rails in the Gulf Country", current availability unknown. I have also referred to Robin Barnes' article 'Railmotor to Laura' which appeared in 'Locomotives International' issue 59 and I wish to thank Norman Drake and Stan Berry for providing further information and photographs following that article.

RM60, successor to the 'Endeavour' on the Normanton line, now restored and seen here displayed at Normanton on 10th June 1998.
                    Photo: Stan Berry.

Classic Motive Power in Australia by Wilf Simms

WESTERN AUSTRALIA

The Western Australia Government Railway placed a number of orders with UK manufacturers as part of their initial 3'6" gauge dieselisation programme First to arrive on the scene were three 129hp Class Z Drewry/Robert Stephenson & Hawthorn 0-6-0DM shunters (Z 1151-1153) of which Z 1151 had the honour to be the first diesel locomotive to enter service on the WAGR October 1953. Rarely seen by enthusiasts, they worked for much of their lives on jetty shunting. All survived into preservation.

Quickly on their heels came eighteen 375hp Class Y yard and branch-line Bo-Bo DE locomotives from Bntish-Thomson-Houston (Y 1101-1118), but for its mainline workings the WAGR placed their reliance on a relatively untested design from the Bowesfield Works, Stockton-on-Tees, of the Beyer Peacock and Metropolitan Vickers Company partnership. The resultant forty-eight 1105hp Class X were constructed 1953-55 with a unique rigid-plate frame and motored axles in the centre, supported by trailing bogies under the long overhang at either end (2-Do-2DE). In service numerous design faults came to light, some due to the locomotives rough-riding, others to the Crossley submarine-type 2-stroke engine. Eventually they settled down to perform useful and reliable service throughout the WAGR network and although withdrawals commenced in 1973 examples were still in operation during the mid-1980s. The first thirty-two (Class X 1001 1032) were without multiple-unit capability when built, the next sixteen (Class XA 1401-1416) had multiple unit equipment and communicating doors fitted at the factory. Subsequently a further ten Class X (1004/06/08/17/18/20/22/24/27/32) were fitted with mu equipment by WAGR from 1963 but did not receive communicating doors. Prototype X 1001 'YALAGONGA' is preserved at the ARHS Museum, Bassendean.

In an attempt to halt mounting costs and low traffic levels WAGR introduced its first lightweight petrol railcars in 1922, taking a big leap forward in 1937 with its Armstrong Whitworth-built Class ADE diesel-electric type, followed by home-built Class ADF (with English Electric equipment) in 1949. No Class ADE has survived but ADF (or Wildflower Class) 495 'BANKSIA' is at Bassendean.

By the early 1950s Perth suburban services were competing

Above: Westrail Class Y 1111 serves as depot shunter at the dual gauge Forrestfield Depot on the outskirts of Perth.

Left: My own favourite Australian diesel - a classic 1950s UK design: Westrail Class XA 1413 'YABAROO' also at Forrestfield on the same date.

with the rapid rise in private car ownership and a radical programme of rail improvement was initiated. Two orders were placed with Cravens of Sheffield for diesel-mechanical railcars, both fitted with twin AEC engines: Class ADG 601-18 for suburban service in 1954 and Class ADH 651-54 for country services (1955-57), the latter modified 1962-63 for suburban use around Perth. Matching control trailers were constructed by WAGR 1961-66. Both Classes were converted to hydraulic drive from the 1970s. All subsequent railcar deliveries have been of local manufacture, the first (Class ADX) from the railway's own workshops being very similar in general design to the Craven examples.

SOUTHERN AUSTRALIA

Rail services centred on Adelaide hub were operated by South Australian Railways until 1975 when they were taken over by the State Transport Authority of South Australia (STA). In 1978 the country lines were transferred to Australian National (formerly Commonwealth) Railways. Two pioneer Bo-Bo DE locomotives (350-351) were constructed by SAR for the 5'3" gauge system at their lslington Workshops in 1949 using English Electric equipment. Both are now preserved. These were followed by what are termed the first ten (900-910) main line diesel locomotives built in Australia. Although a product of SAR's lslington Shops, the equipment again came from English Electric (EE

Left and below: A classic design, much loved by Australian rail enthusiasts, ANR 909 awaits its fate at lslington Works. The view below shows the trailing end of 909.

even allocated works numbers 1849-57). A classic 1588hp single-ended AlA-AlA DE (somewhat more American than English in appearance) they saw intensive use on both passenger and heavy freights. Withdrawn by 1985, some languished at lslington awaiting the torch but by then prototype 900 'LADY NORRIE' had already entered the Mile End Railway Museum. English Electric, realising the potential market in Australia, set up its own factory in Rocklea in the Brisbane suburbs. Its initial production of ten heavy shunting Bo-Bo DE (SAR 800-09) also contained a high degree of UK-design content.

CENTRAL AUSTRALIA

Prior to the completion of the standard gauge system linking all state capitals, Commonwealth Railways consisted mainly of 3'6" gauge trackage of which the Port Augusta-Marree-Alice Springs line is probably the most well known, particularly in its final years when the state of the track led to numerous derailments. To dieselise the system fourteen narrow gauge 850hp units were ordered from Birmingham Carriage & Wagon Company which entered service 1954-55 as Class NSU 51-64. With an AlA-AlA DE arrangement and low axle weight they performed well in traffic, particularly considering the harsh conditions of the area; the final task for many examples being to assist in track recovery after completion of new standard gauge lines to Marree and Alice Springs.

Above: Three Class NSU ended up in the hands of the Pichi Richi Railway Preservation Society at Quorn and were awaiting restoration in 1985. Here the prototype NSU 51 is stored at the rear of their purpose-built depot at Quorn.

Left: A single 3'6" gauge diesel railcar (NDH 1) was purchased from Gloucester Carriage & Wagon in the late 1950s but saw little use, ending its days as an information centre at the Homestead Park Pioneer Museum in Port Augusta. Its position parked amongst the shrubbery makes it difficult to photograph.

Purchased from a Shell Refinery in New South Wales in 1964, DR1 was the only standard gauge diesel locomotive of British build used by Commonwealth Railways. Constructed in 1957 by Ruston & Hornsby, it is a standard industrial 0-4-0DH of the manufacturer's Type 165. It served for some years as works shunter at Port Augusta works and when photographed had been stored since 1975.

NEW SOUTH WALES

The New South Wales Government Railways (now State Rail Authority of New South Wales) commenced its standard gauge dieselisation programme in the early 1950s when it acquired twenty Montreal-built switchers. An order placed around the same time with BTH in England for ten Bo-Bo DE units took somewhat longer to arrive and the first only entered service in 1952, as Class 41 (4101-4110). Construction took place at Metro Cammell's Birmingham works but they were somewhat utilitarian in design, with a central cab flanked on either side by 400hp Paxman engines, not improved

Above: BTH type Bo-Bo DE 4102 at Thirlmere Railway Museum.

Left: 4608 heads the line-up of electric locomotives awaiting their next turn of duty at Enfield, Sydney's main diesel and electric depot.

Below: XP2002 CITY OF ARMIDALE exhibits its InterCity XPT livery in the evening shadows at Sydney Central station.

by later addition of bonnet-mounted filters. All had been retired by the 1985 with 4102 passing into preservationists hands at Thirlmere Railway Museum.

New South Wales was an early exponent of overhead electrification at 1500 volts DC for its suburban services around Sydney and in 1957 extended this to its main line across the Blue Mountains to Lithgow. In preparation, the railway constructed a prototype Co+Co WE of 2700hp in its Chullora workshops using Metrovick equipment, which entered service in 1952 numbered 4501 (renumbered 7100 in 1961). After several months of trials NSWGR placed an order for forty very similar, more powerful (at 3780hp) but less box-like locomotives. As the Class 46 (4601-4640), construction took place at the Scotswood Works of the Metrovick-Beyer Peacock joint company during 1954-55.

Britain had little input in subsequent modern traction orders until 1970 when the Australian firm Comeng designed an XPT or Express Passenger Train based on the successful British Railways HST design. First delivered to SRA in 1981, the units did not find favour with the rail unions, delaying their full introduction. Unlike their UK counterparts which used welded steel, the Comeng version was of stainless steel. A total of fifteen power cars were built 1981-84 (XP2000-2014).

QUEENSLAND

Queensland chose the Cape or 3'6" gauge for its main network, although a standard gauge link now extends from New South Wales to Brisbane. Apart from railcars and the odd shunting locomtive, dieselisation only began in earnest in the early 1950s with an order for ten 'classic' 1290hp English Electric Co-Co DE of Class 1200 (1200-1209). After a short running-in period they were soon in charge of the state's top express passenger services 'The Sunlander' and 'The Inlander', from which much publicity was derived by the UK manufacturers. Constructed in association with Vulcan Foundry in 1953, they remained the only true cab units to operate on Queensland Railways and the class prototype (appropriately named 'The Sunlander') is preserved by the AHRS.

All subsequent diesel orders were placed with Australian builders. QR were obviously pleased with Class 1200 and in 1959 a development, Class 1250, appeared from English Electric's Rocklea Works.

The only other diesel purchased from the UK was a single Class DL 2-6-0DM constructed to a somewhat archaic Queensland Railways design and delivered in 1954 by Robert Stephenson &

Hawthorns. Eventually the DL Class totalled four locomotives of three slightly differing designs. DL1 was constructed at QR's Ipswich Works in 1939 as an 0-6-0 (but quickly modified to 2-6-0DM arrangement) and DL3 and DL4 by Walkers in 1961. The class were popular on lightly laid branches in the north of the country but by 1985 were employed on general duties.

During 1952-54 in an attempt to reduce operating costs and improve local services the Drewry Car Co. supplied twelve 153hp Gardner-engined Class RM1800 diesel-hydraulic railcars and twelve intermediate trailers, intended to be operated in M-T-T-M formation. Motors were RM1800/03-04/07-08/11-12/15-16/19-20/23: the intermediate numbers being taken by the trailers.

The Drewry railcars had been sidelined by 1985 except for RM1811 converted to the Commissioners Inspection Car, and trailer TP1809 transferred to the isolated Normanton-Croydon line on account of its light weight (allowing it to be towed by the then resident railcar RMD93).

Above: Sadly all Class 1200 had been withdrawn by 1985 and stored at Redbank Works where 1209 chalked 'for scrap' awaits its fate.

Left: Odd man out, British-built DL2 FORSAYTH outside Townsville Depot.

RM1803 heads a line of Drewry railcars put out to grass at Redbank Diesel Works.

VICTORIA

Victorian Railways, just to be different, chose the broad 5'3" or 1600mm gauge and electrified her first suburban service on 1500 volts DC overhead wire system in 1918. Later it was decided to extend electrification to freight and shunting duties within the suburban area and after constructing two steeple-cab locomotives a series of ten box-body units appeared, both types having General Electric equipment. These sufficed until 1949 when the decision was taken to electrify the Gippsland line, which served brown coal deposits which at that time were essential for electricity generation. An order was placed with English Electric, in conjunction with Vulcan Works, for 17 (later extended to 25) 2400hp Class L Co-Co WE (1150-1174) of very similar design to those built for RENFE and Indian Railways. The first examples entered service around Melbourne in 1953.

In the diesel field the UK had little involvement other than the supply of 10 British Railways Class 08 lookalikes (Class F301-319, later renumbered 201-210) constructed by English Electric at Dick Kerr Works in 1951. Six examples were also supplied to the State Electricity Commission of Victoria 1951/53; these subsequently passed to Victorian Railways between 1957 and 1959 to become F211-216.

Early suburban electric trains were formed of converted or 'swing door' steam stock and purpose-built but still traditional 'Tait' stock which sufficed until the 1950s when the rapid expansion of Melbourne, increase in commuting and necessity to replace life-expired stock became apparent. Lack of capacity within railway workshops meant that the order was placed with outside contractors, the Gloucester Railway Carriage & Wagon Company supplying 90 motor coaches of 'Harris' type (Harris was a former Chairman of Commissioners for Victorian

Traffic on the Gippsland line did not develop as intended and surplus locomotives allowed retirement of the earlier American-equipped E Class. L1159, with L1158 in the background, awaits its next turn of duty at South Dynon (Melbourne) Depot.

Left: F216, a former State Electricity Commission locomotive at Newport Works. Note the addition of protective bars below the frame.

Below: English Electric built F201 stored at South Dynon (Melbourne) Depot.

Railways) with English Electric equipment; Commonwealth Engineering and Martin & King for 120 matching trailers. The first two motor coaches were imported complete, the remainder as kits of parts which were assembled at Newport Works. The first 7-car unit (M-T-T-M+CT-T-M) in blue and gold livery entered service in March 1956 and all deliveries were completed by 1959. Subsequently a further 226 coaches were constructed in Australia.

Note: All photographs in Victoria taken December 1984.

A line of Harris stock at MTA Jolimont Workshops with Gloucester-built driving motor 556M at the head. The MTA or Metropolitan Transit Authority of Victoria was formed in 1983 to operate the former services of the Victorian Railways around Melbourne and the Metropolitan Tramways Board.

Foreign Exchange - the Soviet-built Class M62 Co-Co *by Paul Catchpole*

In 1964 two prototypes of a new Co-Co locomotive design, intended as an export product, were built at the Lugansk Locomotive Works in the Ukraine. (Lugansk town and the works were renamed as Voroshilovgrad during the Soviet era). The prototypes were built with broad gauge bogies and remained in the USSR, but the first series production locomotives were for Hungary, where

Drawing of the M62: Lugansk Locomotive Works, courtesy of ČSD

there was a genuine shortage of heavy goods engines. The M62 designation for the class originates with the MÁV (Hungarian State Railways) numbering system and follows in succession from the M61 series allocated to the American-style Nohab Bo-Bos.

The USSR had large reserves of oil from wells in central Asia which it supplied to the Communist Bloc countries, using the notional revenue to offset against the exports they were obliged to provide in return, usually in the form of high quality manufactured products. Already, captured wartime class 52 'Kriegsloks' 2-10-0s had been sold back to eastern European railways, modified to burn Russian oil and for which an additional charge was made for the necessary re-conversion back to standard gauge from the Russian

5' gauge (1524mm). Following this with a heavy diesel locomotive requiring more Russian oil ensured a continuity of demand.

From 1964 to 1976 at least 8,281 M62s were built, 2,438 locos for the standard gauge and 1,926 for the broad gauge, plus 3,917 units for double and triple-unit locomotives. The break-down of where they went is shown in Table 1.

Technical Characteristics

Each locomotive or unit is powered by a Kolomna type 2-stroke V-12 supercharged diesel motor, type 14D40, with a power output of 1470kW at 750 rpm (1735kW when fitted with a silencer). In operation, two turbochargers driven by exhaust gas and one with a

Table 1:				Countries to which the M62s were supplied		
Country	Admin-istration	Soviet Desig-nation	Local Class	Gauge	Dates Supplied	Quantity
Cuba	FC	M62K	61	1435mm	1974-75	20
Czechoslovakia	ČSD	M62	T679.1 / 781	1435mm	1966-73, 1979	574
	ČSD	M62	T679.5 / 781.8	1524mm	1966	25
	Industrial	M62	T679.5	1524mm	1969	2
DDR	DR	M62	V200 / 120	1435mm	1966	378
	Industrial	M62	V200 / 120	1435mm	1970s	18
Hungary	MÁV	M62	M62	1435mm	1965-74	270
	MÁV	M62	M62	1524mm	1978	18
	GySEV	M62	M62	1435mm	1972	6
Mongolia	MTZ	M62UM	M62UM	1524mm	1989-90	13
	MTZ	2M62UM	2M62UM	1524mm	1980-87	66
North Korea	ZMI	K62	LH01	1435mm	1967-69	47
	Industrial	K62	LH01	1435mm	1967-69	2
	local production		Kumsong	1435mm	1975-?	?
Poland	PKP	M62	ST44	1435mm	1965-68	1114
	PKP	M62	ST44	1524mm	1965-68	68
	Industrial	M62	ST44	1435mm	1965-68	9
USSR	SZD	M62	M62	1524mm	1970-76	1800
	SZD	2M62	2M62	1524mm	1976-87	1261
	SZD	2M62U	2M62U	1524mm	1987-?	99+
	SZD	3M62U	3M62U	1524mm	1986-?	355+
	Industrial	M62	M62	1524mm		? (probably included in M62 total)

mechanical drive from the engine, clear the exhaust from the cylinders when the exhaust valves are uncovered at bottom dead centre of the piston stroke and they replenish the fuel/air mixture as the piston rises. The motor drives a GP312 DC generator feeding the current for six 193kW air-cooled ED107 traction motors. The diesel motor is water-cooled, with an additional control system for regulating the lubricating oil temperature. The pivoting bogies famously lack lateral movement in the centre axle and the minimum radius of track they can take is (officially) 128 m. Axle weight is 19.4 tonnes, total weight 116.5 tonnes, maximum speed 100 km/h and tractive effort 350 kN. The twin and triple units are slightly heavier with 20t axle weight (21t for 2M62U and 3M62U) and the later models have modified bogies.

Hungarian loco M62.090 had worked quite a long way into Slovakia when it was seen at Zvolen on 3rd August 1994. Photo: Martin Nový

Table 2:	Common Nicknames
Czechoslovakia	Sergej (from a political figure), also Petrolin (in parts of Slovakia)
DDR	Taiga-Trommel (from the sound of the engine)
Hungary	Gagarin (the 1960s cosmonaut)
Poland	Szergej
USSR	Mashka

Hungary

The first exported locomotives produced at Lugansk went to Hungary in 1965 and the supply of standard gauge locos continued until 1967, by which time 288 had been taken into MÁV stock (M62.001-288). Ten more were added to these in 1987 when the Hungarians bought surplus locos off the ČSD. The GySEV's six M62s were delivered in 1972, nos. M62.901-906, and the broad gauge MÁV examples were received in 1978, nos. M62.501-518 stationed at Zahony.

In 2002 127 'Szergej' Co-Cos remained in stock, including 12 of Zahony's 5' gauge locos and M62.001 allocated to Szolnok but assured of a future in preservation. Two locos have been modernised and were renumbered M62.301/302.

A double-headed ČSD freight shakes Ostrov nad Ohři station at 17:50 on 17th July 1986. T679.1237 is leading with T679.1464 behind.
Photo: Zdeněk Kačena.

Czechoslovakia

In 1966 the ČSD took delivery of fifty M62s, twenty-five class T679.1 standard gauge locos and twenty five class T679.5 for the broad gauge line from Maťovce to Haniska pri Košiciach. The standard gauge examples were divided between Zvolen in central Slovakia and Brno and Nové Zámky for working freights from the Hungarian border to Česká Třebová. The next ten followed in 1967 and were allocated to Praha Vršovice depot for working south to České Budějovice, after which subsequent deliveries resulted in their dispersal throughout the former Czechoslovakia. Some minor modifications were made for compliance with ČSD braking equipment and from 1968 silencers were fitted.

The standard gauge variants were renumbered around 1990 to class 781 and the broad gauge to 781.8, retaining their running numbers.

The effect of the arrival of the T679.1 was to reduce the depen-

dency on heavy goods steam locomotives, however, they were also used on passenger trains, including expresses. As they were not fitted with train heating equipment, some special vehicles were constructed using the boilers of withdrawn class 310 tank locomotives so that passenger operation could continue during the harsh winter months.

Due to a political exercise where one loco was numbered T679.1400, the numbering of ČSD standard gauge locos perhaps should be clarified. The re-numbered loco was T679.1354 and the number remained vacant, while the numbers T679.1375 - T679.1399 also remained unused, until seventeen broad gauge locos were converted to standard gauge following electrification of their route. Thus, although a total of 599 locos were purchased by the ČSD, the number 781.600 is valid for the preserved example, formerly T679.1600. To further complicate matters, four

Slovak 781s were converted to broad gauge for use on maintenance trains, nos. 781.281/282/317 & 373, renumbered 781.825-828 (T679.5026/5027 were the two industrial locos in Slovakia). They were the most numerous single ČSD locomotive class.

At the time of their introduction fuel oil was cheap but high consumption became a problem after the collapse of the Communist system in 1989 when prices rose. Perhaps greater though was the cost in damage to the track caused by the heavy weight and lack of side-play in the centre axles of the bogies, so with greater independence from Soviet influence a start on withdrawals was made prior to the 'velvet divorce' of the Czech and Slovak Republics on 1st January 1993. The last few working in Slovkia were withdrawn in the late 1990s but four locos lingered on at Sokolov in the Czech Republic until 30th November 2002, working coal trains from Cheb to Arzberg in Germany.

Since withdrawals started some locomotives have been overhauled and modified for sale to private operators in Germany and

for North Korea. Preserved examples are ČD 781.529/578/600 and ŽS 781.168/312/368.

Poland

A large number of M62s went to Poland, 1114 of them becoming PKP nos. ST44-101 to ST44-1113 and ST44-1500. The latter was carried on the same bogies as were fitted to later multiple-unit locos Another 68 broad gauge locos were delivered for the Hutniczo - Siarkowej line and nine were obtained for industrial service. The PKP fitted large headlights just above buffer beam level, as generally seen on other Polish locomotive types. The Polish Co-Cos were painted in a green livery with a yellow panel below the windscreen, orange across the front at buffer beam level and black bogies, frames and fuel tank.

By the end of the 1980s withdrawals of the ST44s had started but as at 1st January 2002 the PKP still had 190 "Gagarins" rostered to twelve depots. Another forty-nine were in the stock of the Linie Hutnicza Szerokotorowa and running in the firm's own livery.

Six locos withdrawn in 1998 were sold to Germany, five going to Import Transport Logistic GmbH numbered V200.001-003/005 and 120.004 and one other for OHE as no. 120.004. Nine more were sold off to a private operator in Poland during 1999 and 2000. As detailed later, seventeen locos were overhauled and exported to North Korea in 2000/2001.

East Germany (DDR)

The DR was supplied with 378 M62s in 1966. The East Germans numbered them as class V200, later reclassified into series 120 and after unification again reclassified as series 220. Another eighteen were supplied to industrial concerns in the 1970s. Since withdrawn examples have become available from German and other railways from the late 1990s, the quantity in industrial service or private operation has risen dramatically, especially locomotives purchased by private companies for leasing out. At least twelve locomotives have been preserved, eleven ex-DR and one ex-Braunkohlenkombinat Geiseltal.

USSR

Apart from the two prototypes, the SZD did not take delivery of M62s until 1970 and from 1976 onwards only the the 2M62 twin unit variants were taken into stock. Numbers were M62.1003-1723 and 2M62.0001-1261 (2522 individual units) The twins were not just equipped for multiple-unit working but had corridor connections at the inner ends.

From 1986 an improved version of the twin unit and a triple-unit went into production, the 2M62U and 3M62U, with improved bogies. They also had the cabs blanked off at the inner end and used for the loco's batteries to enable larger quantities of fuel and sand to be carried (but only one cab blanked off on the inner unit)! The 3M62U was used on the Oktyabrskaya and Zabaikalskaya Railways. Numbers were 2M62U.0001-0392 and 3M62U.0001-0104. With the break-up of the Soviet Union the M62s and 2M62/2M62Us were inherited by the railway systems of the newly-independent states. Latvia also purchased 32 redundant M62s from Germany. Numerous further variants were created by modernisation and rebuilding, most notable of which must be Azerbaijan's class E2M62 created by converting eight twin units to electric traction.

Mongolia

Mongolin Tömör Zam (Mongolian Railways) purchased 66 twin-unit 2M62UMs from 1980-87, and only later in 1989-90 obtained thirteen

Broad gauge Russian 'Mashka' M62.1444 in charge of a heavy goods train at Leningrad on 27th July 1982. Photo: Petr David.

single units of type M62UM. The Mongolian livery is green with two thin yellow lines round the body, red embellishments on the front and light grey for the roof and below frame level. The railway through Ulan Bator is an important link between Russia and China and the locomotives are used on all types of traffic.

North Korea

Forty-nine locomotives designated type K62 were exported to North Korea 1967-69. Two of the locos were placed in industrial service and the remainder went into service with North Korea's railways (Zosun Minzuzni Inmingonghoagug) as class LH01. In 1992 North Korea purchased another two locos and a further five in 1995, presumably obtained second-hand. One Korean locomotive from the original K62 batch was converted to electric traction.

With the re-unification of Germany a large number of DBAG (ex-DR) class 220s were being withdrawn in the 1990s and thirty-one of these were sold to North Korea 1996-97, DBAG running

When the Hungarians celebrated 150 years of railways the Ukrainian State Railways were able to send a standard gauge UŽ representative, M62.1607, pictured here taking part in the parade at Budapest-Angyalföld station on 13th July 1996. Photo: Günter Koch.

'A present of loyalty to the Great Leader'. 'Workers of the Chollima Kim Jong Tae Electric Locomotive Plant made a 2,500hp diesel engine "Kumsong" ...upholding the banner of the three revolutions'. (As pictured in DPRKorea Monthly, October 1975).
Below: Workers fix a plate to loco no. 8004.

nos. 008, 043, 048, 086, 087, 114, 119, 159, 180, 211, 219, 234, 289, 290, 292, 296, 305, 317-319, 322, 332, 334, 335, 342, 345, 362, 368, 371, 372, and 375.

Another six second-hand locomotives were shipped out from Gdynia on 8th May 2000, ex-PKP class ST44, running nos. 103, 152, 325, 518, 649 and 673, overhauled and exported in their PKP livery. A further ten locos followed in October 2000. Three of these were Slovak ex-ČSD locomotives nos. 781.826-828, re-numbered M-62-1 to M-62-3, Lugansk works nos. 1191/1971, 0905/1970, and 1247/1971 respectively. The ex-ŽSR locos were repainted olive green with a narrow yellow band around the lower part of the body and red flashes below the cab windows and on the snowploughs. Bogies, frames and fuel tanks were repainted black. The other seven locomotives in the shipment were ex-PKP ST44s nos. 072, 549, 840, 929, 937, 947 and 999. In November 2001 ST44s 595, 641, and 678 were exported in company with Hungarian ex-MÁV M62 110 and an ex-DB V160. PKP ST44-1007 was also exported to North Korea, at an unknown time. (Export data by courtesy of Polish magazine 'Świat kolei').

North Korea has followed its own path as much as possible over the last half a century and decided to manufacture its own 2,500hp version of the K62, designated the 'Kumsong' class. Production started in 1975 at the Kim Jong Tae Electric Locomotive Plant (formerly known as the West Pyongyang Railway Plant). How many were produced is unknown.

Kumsong no. 8002 is preserved in the Museum of the Three Revolutions in Pyongyang.

'Kumsong' M62s are amongst other locomotives under construction at the Kim Jong Tae Electric Locomotive Plant in the mid-1970s. This picture is from the Democratic People's Republic of Korea Monthly, December 1976 issue, taken by Chon Sung Bok.
Photos on this page are courtesy of Nicholas Pertwee.

Cuba

The Ferrocarriles de Cuba's first six M62K Co-Cos arrived in 1974 and another fourteen in 1975. The 'K' after M62 was for 'Kuba', where they were numbered in class 61 as nos. 61 601 to 61 620. The locos differed from the European locomotives as they had to be able to operate in a tropical climate, requiring changes to the cooling system. Some Americanisation was neccessary to conform to Cuban railway stock, including centre couplings and control systems. A minor but visually obvious addition was the American style illuminated light boxes for the loco numbers carried either side of the front of the locomotive.

The M62Ks were stationed at Havana, Cienfuegos and Santa Clara. Little information is available about the work they performed but it seems they were set aside without lasting as long as might have been expected, being prone to overheating and fires. On 29th January 1975, after the initial batch of locomotives were delivered, President Fidel Castro drove 61 602 which thus became known as "Fidel's Sergej". For this reason it was selected for preservation in Havana's railway museum, and is believed to be in working order.

One of the later versions of the twin units, 2M62U-0289, at Kolomiya, Ukraine in October 1994. Photo: Ian Button.

Made in the DDR -
East German Electric Locomotives Still at Work in China
The LEW Hennigsdorf Class EL1 150t Bo-Bo-Bo WE - *by Nicholas Pertwee*

Background

The EL1 was the largest and heaviest industrial electric locomotive produced by LEW and the only 6-axle example. The 150-ton Bo-Bo-Bo sweeper inherited from AEG was a three unit articulated engine with the main pantographs mounted on the fore and aft decking of the centre unit. It resembled the various Škoda articulated engines of, for example, Classes 37E1, 2 & 3 in use at Anshan, Fuxin and Fushun today and as at the middle of 1953 had been manufactured "in large numbers" in the DDR for use domestically and in other countries. Later that year this old design was portrayed, together with the newly-introduced EL2, as being part of LEW's own standardisation programme to meet the increasing transportation needs of the mining industry. However, despite apparently proven performance on track often subject to distortion and sinking due to unstable track-beds, which ran counter to the idea that a 3-unit articulated 150-tonner was somehow more prone to derailments, the conversion of the old design to the 2-unit EL1 that can be seen at work in China today was already being hinted at in August 1955 when a new development of the electrical and mechanical parts was said to be 'still' under way. This development, which finally resulted something over two years later in a locomotive consisting of two back-to-back units slung over a central Bo-bogie, with short bonnets fore and aft and the main pantographs mounted on the roof above the driver's cab at each end, was in practice to cater for the burgeoning demand

from the USSR and it was with that in mind that the new version was produced. Of the 930 new-style EL1s made, no less than 809 went to the USSR.

This raises the interesting - though in the case of China perhaps not directly relevant - question of how many completely new EL1s in the old 3-unit form were actually made, rather than merely refurbished, by LEW. Information on this subject is somewhat contradictory. The section in 'Zeitzeugnisse' on the EL1 tells us that 3 old 3-unit 150-tonners were overhauled and delivered to two mining concerns in the DDR between 1951 and 1953, though there are two other sources that put the number at 5 in the same period. Despite this discrepancy the reference is almost certainly to the same old-form locomotives in each case, and the most likely answer is that no new locomotives in the old form were made by LEW, though the intention at first had surely been to carry on with developments of the old AEG design. This after all became the standard format used by Škoda, and examples are still at work in China today. Operational needs in the USSR must have made a new more powerful design necessary almost from the start and it was this form which was exported there from the beginning of 1958 when two test units were delivered for evaluation. It was also displayed as a model at that year's Leipzig New Year's Fair in the LEW Pavilion. Though 'Referenzen' (a record produced by LEW of deliveries 1949-1966) has the date as 1957 for the export of the first two examples, I do not believe this means that there were two isolated 3-unit EL1s of the old design sent to the USSR, but that this is a reference to the same two new-style EL1s as mentioned above, the ones sent there for assessment. It is more likely that 1957 refers in this case to the date on the works plate, rather in the same way as the first 16 EL2s exported to China, though having 1956-dated works plates, are recorded in 'Referenzen' as having been exported only in 1957.

Exports to China of the new 2-unit EL1 began in 1960 and though 121 of them went there, there is probably only one place, Fuxin, where they can be really well seen at work and in some ways they are a rather elusive locomotive. Part of the reason for this is that their use is generally restricted to main lines - the only exception being Fuxin - which are less accessible than the lines leading into

One of Benxi's locomotive allocation, no. 1515, in a clean condition.
The specification plate can be discerned, affixed below the cabside number.

Despite the fact that the front and rear bogies are of the same construction on the EL1, it is possible to distinguish between which is intended to be the front and back of the locomotive as the axles are in some cases marked from 1 to 6 above the axlebox, on the spring. Using this as a guide it is apparent that the right hand side has a narrow louvre behind the cab, in two parts straddling the upper and lower parts of the body casing. The immacculate no. 1551 illustrating these features was photographed at Qitaihe.

open-cast mines, but perhaps of more significance is the fact that at Fushun at any rate, which had the largest allocation, they have been put aside and are no longer in use. Not a single LEW locomotive of any class was seen at work there in the summer of 2002, which makes it a unique location, and only a storage area containing 21 EL1s was found. Where the other 20 or so are is a matter for conjecture, as is the purpose to which they might now be put. Their external condition is still good in most cases as the last were only put out to grass in October 2001 and many are shrouded in tarpaulins, but it would only be speculation to suggest that they might find further employment elsewhere. Their tasks at Fushun are now handled by other 150-tonners, either their Chinese-built equivalent, the ZG150, or 37E-class Škodas. At Anshan too other EL1s have been 'stored', to put it euphemistically, while Hegang has also abandoned at least 4 of its allocation, so that most places now only use a relatively small number. With the total in regular use across all its locations now down to probably 30, it has become something of a rara avis.

CLASS EL1 150t Bo-Bo-Bo WE ALLOCATION SITES AND NUMBERS						
Works No. Group	Date Built	Total Built	Location	Estimate per Location	Seen - of Which >>>	Seen & Identified
9211-9250	1960/61	40	Anshan	16		
			Benxi/Waitoushan	16		
			Fuxin	2		
			Fushun	12		
9346-9369	1961	24	Anshan	13		
			Fushun	11		
13228-13257	1970	30	Anshan	6		
			Benxi/Waitoushan	6		
			Fushun	12		
			Fuxin	5		
			Qitaihe	1		
13258-13264	1971	7	Benxi/Waitoushan	2		
			Hegang	4		
			Qitaihe	1		
16585-16604	1980	20	Fushun	5		
			Fuxin	5		
			Hegang	6		
			Qitaihe	4		
TOTALS	1960-80	121	Anshan	35	29	8
			Benxi/Waitoushan	10	5 (1)	2 (0)
			Fushun	40	36	17
			Fuxin	20	16	9
			Hegang	10	10	6
			Qitaihe	6	6	6
				[121]	[102]	[48]

Sources/Notes:

1. LEW Works Lists by Huetter and Merte (for works number groups);
2. Industrial Locomotives and its Amendment Lists;
3. Personal Observations;
4. 'Seen & Identified' refers to locomotives positively identified as to works number and/or date from their works plates.

At the same time though, apart from Fuxin where they were in poor external condition when last seen in the summer of 2002, EL1s still at work at Anshan, Benxi, Hegang and Qitaihe are very well maintained and there is no reason to suppose that they will be discarded any time soon. Particularly at those locations (Benxi, Hegang and Qitaihe) where there are no other types of 150-tonners to call on as replacements, their future must be bright.

The following table shows how the 121 EL1s exported to China were, or in cases where hard and fast data is not available but implied or assumed might have been, allocated.

Construction and External Features

The EL1s at work in China display few external features to differentiate between such variants as might have been built. The only ones that have been seen to carry a specifications plate to give a clue to this are those at Benxi which are designated EL1/06. Contrary to the EL2, of which 1380 examples were built in some 20 variants over 35 years and supplied to users in 5 countries including the DDR itself, the EL1 was only sent to the USSR and China and had a shorter manufacturing life. It is not unlikely, therefore, that it remained more consistent in its design and that for China at least there may only have been one model.

There are only minor differences to be observed in the number and distribution of the hatches and louvres along either side of the Chinese EL1s, irrespective of whether they come from the earliest examples at Fuxin which date from 1960 and 1961 or are from the 1980 batch stationed at Hegang or Qitaihe. Side collectors are only regularly carried at Fuxin, on the fore and aft bonnets, and while there are traces of a support for this feature in this position visible on, literally, a couple of others elsewhere, the EL1 is primarily a main line locomotive in China. Pictures and diagrams of EL1s made for the USSR on the other hand show brackets extending out from the roof of the cab to support side collectors and another area where those sent to China differ is in their lack of the supplementary cooling device for the compressor. The dual-control provision which enables 2 locomotives to work in tandem is restricted to the earlier, 1960/61, models sent to China which means effectively Fuxin and a small number at Anshan.

Departing from the practice where riveting was used in the construction of heavy industrial locomotives, the bogies, underframe and superstructure of the EL1 were welded. A two-part underframe was used to accommodate the mass of electrical equipment needed and provide better running qualities. Electrical rheostatic brakes were employed permitting operation on long gradients and provision made for dual-control to increase the tractive effort. The EL1 was made for both broad and standard gauges and the versions sent to the USSR and China differed mainly in the height and type of the couplings and the position of the current collectors. The driver's control panel was situated for either left- or right-hand running.

The three bogies are connected by short and compensating couplings to transmit the horizontal tractive and impact forces, and the vertical forces. The leading and rear bogies are of the same construction to facilitate replacement without concern for whether they come from the front or back of the locomotive; they are supported flexibly on the axles, with the leaf springs above the axle bearings connected by a compensating spring. The middle bogie is supported rigidly and has no compensating spring.

Despite the fact that the leading and rear bogies are of the same construction, there are cases where the axle numbers are painted onto the axle box, which enables one to distin-

SPECIFICATIONS

Category	Per Zeitzeugnisse	Specifications Plate
Wheel Arrangement	Bo-Bo-Bo	
Length over Couplers	21,320 mm	21,045 mm
Kingpin Centre	2 x 6,200 mm	
Bogie Centre	2,800 mm	
Wheel Diameter	1,120 mm	
Gauge	1,520/1,435mm	
Height to Pantograph Blade	4,850 mm	4,045 mm*
Width		2,150 mm
Weight	160/150 t	150 t
Maximum Speed	65 km/h	
Hourly Output	2,100 kW	2,100 kW
Speed at Hourly Output	29.7 km/h	
Tractive Effort at Hourly Output	242 kN	24,700 kg
Continuous Rating	1,740 kW	1,740 kW
Speed at Continuous Rating	33 km/h	
Tractive Effort at Continuous Rating	184 kN	18,900 kg
Maximum Tractive Effort	471 kN	45 t
Voltage and Current System	1,500 V DC	1,500 V DC
Electric Brakes	Resistance Brakes	
Minimum Radius		80 m

Notes:
(1) Technical details in the column headed 'Per Zeitzeugnisse' are taken from that publication, pp. 104/105.
(2) The column headed 'Specifications Plate' lists the details carried by EL1 1516 at Benxi and refers to sub-class EL1/06. This plate, which contains the principal technical details, is typical of others of its type but where the EL1 is concerned is only to be found on locomotives stationed at Benxi. It is in Chinese except for the maker's name which has been left as LEW Hennigsdorf.
(3) 4,045 mm* - in this case the measurement is simply the height of the locomotive, i.e. excluding the pantograph.

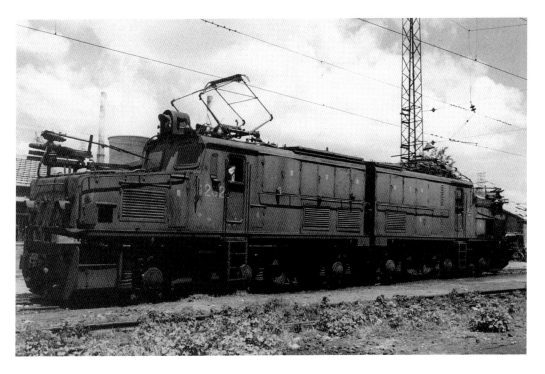

EL1 no. 9232 at Fuxin. The small open hatch by the louvre at the nearer end is a feature of the earlier locos which was enlarged later, as can be seen in the picture of no. 1551 on page 70.

guish between the front and back of the locomotive and thus to allocate alterations to louvres and hatches to one side of it or the other.

References

AEG Mitteilungen, *January & February 1940*
Elektrische Bahnen, *October & December 1943*
Eisenbahntechnik, *July & October 1953*
Deutsche Eisenbahntechnik,
      August 1955, March & August 1958, September 1959
Zeitzeugnisse, Part II

Above: The specification plates are only carried on the EL1s at Benxi, in this case locomotive no. 1516 (works no. 13264/1971) of sub-class EL1/06.

Left: The 1960 works plate of LEW no. 9230 at Benxi, where the running number corresponds to the works noumber.

Immaculately turned out with white tyres, class EL1 Co-Co-Co no. 1505 handles a long train of bogie mineral wagons at Hegang in 2001.

Made in the DDR -
East German Electric Locomotives Still at Work in China
The LEW Hennigsdorf Class EL2 100t Bo-Bo WE - *by Nicholas Pertwee*

Background

The 100-ton Bo-Bo sweeper locomotive inherited by LEW from AEG underwent no radical design change of the kind that transformed the 150-tonner. the EL1, from a three-unit to a two-unit locomotive but over its long manufacturing life it appeared in some 20 variants which differed, externally at any rate, mainly in the position of the main pantographs, the number of ventilation louvres provided and whether or not the locomotive was fitted with dual-control equipment. The following table shows the numbers built and the countries in which they were used.

TOTAL PRODUCED AND USER COUNTRIES		
COUNTRY	YEARS	QUANTITY
DDR	1952-1988	681
USSR	1957-1970	245
Bulgaria	1960-1987	206
China	**1957-1984**	**186**
Poland	1958-1987	62
TOTAL	1952-1987	1380

Source: Zeitzeugnisse, Part II, p. 98

It has been possible to tabulate the main technical specifications of eight of these variants from data provided in Zeitseugnisse and from publicity material put out by Hennigsdorf. Where the EL2/18, one of the two versions of the EL2 sent to China, is concerned, the Chinese specifications plate provides two points of amplification of the official Hennigsdorf data, with the width of the locomotive and the minimum negotiable radius. In the case of the other version exported to China. the EL2/23. Such technical details as are available have all come from the Chinese specifications plate. The table in question appears at the end of this section.

From the table it is possible to see how the EL2/18 stands out from the other EL2 variants. It is the only one with a significantly different 'Height of Coupling above Top of Rail' measurement (880mm compared to 1,020mm, or 1,055mm in the case of the EL2/05 for the USSR), which would no doubt be shared with the EL2/23 if the appropriate data was to hand, nor is it fitted with dual-control equipment. The absence of this latter feature fits in for example with the earliest two batches sent to China, those of 1956 to Hegang (actually exported in 1957) and 1961 to Anshan.

LEW 1965 publicity material for the EL2 describes it as follows: "Features of the locomotive type EL2 are the twin articulated bogies and the underframe executed in all-welded construction of profile girders and plates with its rigid superstructures and detachable hoods. This construction distinguished itself by especially good running qualities which make it especially suitable for the tracks in open-cast mines that are mostly temporarily laid. The different executions differ mainly in the electrical equipment in the buffer and draw gear, in the pneumatic brake, and in the arrangement of current collectors". It adds that they are equipped with multiple unit control, enabling two locomotives to be operated in tandem, and a slow-running device for continuous loading under an excavator. Extremes of temperature from -40C to +35C can be accommodated.

As I have used the differences in the construction of the front and rear bogies to distinguish between the right and left-hand side of the locomo-

A broadside view of EL2 no. 113 at Anshan. Features to note: Two roof-mounted pantographs; long roof overhang; X-shaped impression on cabside panel for strengthening; this batch of locomotives is not fitted for dual control nor does it have the supplementary cooling apparatus for the compressor. This is fitted at the front end of the locomotive in later models, the front end being identifiable by the leading bogie having a compensating spring between the two leaf springs. Note also, numbers on the axle boxes to distinguish between leading and trailing bogies. The right-hand side is shown here, with the collector at the front, which matches the positioning seen on the later 72xx series running numbers at Anshan. The pattern of louvres and hatches differed in later models.

Nos. 7335 (17355/1981), left and 7349 (17349/1981), below are representative of the 37-strong fleet of EL2s working at Pingzhuang, among which is a smaller number with 67xx-series running numbers dating from 1980, which are of similar appearance. No. 7335 is running rear-end first and so showing its left-hand side, while no. 7349 is displaying its right-hand side. The difference in the arrangement of louvres and hatches on the two sides is clear.

tive when pointing out certain features, it is worth quoting in part the explanation about the bogies from the same publicity material. There inter alia we are told that "The two bogies are connected to each other by means of a short and compensating coupling from which favourable conditions result with regard to the running qualities and the utilisation of the adhesion weight. The short coupling transmits the horizontal longitudinally directed tractive and shock forces, the compensating coupling vertical forces being directed across the longitudinal axle (sic) of the locomotive from one bogie to the other". It goes on to say that

the front bogie rests flexibly and the rear bogie rigidly on the axles, with the leaf springs of the front bogie above the axle bearings connected to each other by means of a compensating spring. This latter piece of information enables one to distinguish between the leading and trailing bogies, and thus identify the front and back of the locomotive and the relative positions of such prominent external features as the side current collectors.

From the published sources quoted earlier in the section on the EL1, which overlap to a large extent with the EL2 (as these two models came to represent the standard types used in open-cast mines and their associated railway systems from the early- to mid-1950s) one sees plans and illustrations of a design generally uniform in appearance and dimensions. The dates of these sources provide, however, a clue to what seems to have been the main departure externally from the pre-war and earlier post-war examples. This is in the positioning of the main pantographs, where at least by 1956 (as can be seen from the earliest locomotives at Hegang) they have been moved from the fore and aft decking to the cab roof.

This was the pattern also seen in the two EL2s specially adapted for use with motorised tipper wagons for the USSR in 1964.

None of the EL2s in China have anything other than roof-mounted pantographs and in this context the photograph in Zeitseugnisse of an EL2 bearing the already factory-applied running number 7405 (probably works number 14023 of 1974) being loaded aboard ship for the voyage to China is interesting as it illustrates well the lack of the heavy mounting on the fore-decking which would be needed to support a main pantograph, though the lighter base for a side collector is present.

LOCATION NOTES

There follow brief notes on the various sites where EL2s can be seen at work.

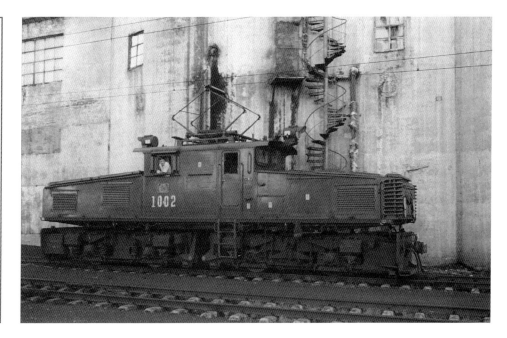

The four EL2s working at Qitaihe are all from the last 1984 batch but unlike the two at Fuxin, which have two pantographs on the cab roof and side current collectors, they have only one roof-mounted pantograph and lack side collectors. In this respect they resemble the 23xx-series EL2s at Hegang which are also used only for main-line running, there being no side-wire sections on the mine railway system at Qitaihe which would necessitate side current collectors.

ANSHAN (Liaoning Province)

Most observations of EL2s at work at Anshan have centred round the steelworks complex where probably 12 or so work. Access is restricted and it is difficult to examine them closely in the time usually allowed, and an added problem in trying to assess how many are there is presented by the fact that they do not usually emerge from the steel-mill area onto the main mine railway line, unlike the EL1s or the Skodas also operated by Anshan Steel Corporation. There are however a number of iron-ore mines around Anshan and some of these have their own separate allocations of a variety of electric locomotives, including EL2s. A visit to one of these mines in the summer of 2002 revealed EL2s at work having running numbers in the 1xx, 72xx and 74xx series and it is not unlikely that others may yet be found in other Anshan mines. Thus, the number of EL2s given for Anshan in the Site and Number Allocation Table is not regarded as excessive. It may indeed be conservative, and there seems little doubt that the Anshan complex in its various forms was the recipient of the largest number of EL2s out of the total 186 sent to China.

Anshan also has the distinction of having the oldest (1961) batch of EL2s in China apart from Hegang and the large scale of its operations required additions to this early fleet at regular intervals up to 1981.

BENXI/WAITOUSHAN (Liaoning Province)

EL2s at Benxi itself work primarily on routine transportation duties and are used on the lines linking three large marshalling yards, which takes them past but not into the main steelworks area. They also cross the river on the electrified bridge down from the electric maintenance depot to visit the vicinity of another steel mill and a steel pipe factory, and sometimes a cement factory which lies in the opposite direction. Benxi has an associated iron-ore mine at Waitoushan which is about one hour away by train and a variety of electric locomotives, including EL2s, work there. The EL2s work down from the mine to a marshalling yard next to the national railway system's main line, where their trains are picked up by Benxi-based DF4-type Co-Co heavy diesels. It is

not yet known exactly how many electric locomotives of any type work at Waitoushan but at least three EL2s have been seen there so far.

As far as their external features are concerned, EL2s at Benxi share the characteristics of locomotives from the same construction batches as seen at other places. There are however two interesting minor features. One is the Q1 DDR plate they carry, not seen so far on any other EL2 anywhere except on a single example at Hegang, and the other is a fine example of one of the works plates that have the year of manufacture not in its conventional form but using only the salient two digits of it in, in this case, the form 72xx. The former denotes 'Erste Qualitaet' or 'Erste Qualitaetsarbeit', a quality achievement standard awarded to LEW products. Zeitzeugnisse (7) lists the awards that were given to LEW products, and it is reasonable to assume that this badge was something of this nature, possibly indicating receipt of the Ehrentitel "Betrieb der ausgezeichneten Qualitaetsarbeit".

FUXIN (Liaoning Province)

As far as visits to Fuxin have been able to establish, the EL2 is not a common locomotive there and there are only two of them in regular use. These, together with one presently dumped example and one other seen some time ago (but not recently, which leads one to believe that it has been scrapped) all come from the last 1984 batch and have 84xx date-based running numbers. This seems to suggest that it was something of an afterthought that caused Fuxin to order them. Even so, their use is restricted. Despite being fitted with side collectors they do not go down into Haizhou Pit but instead work heavy slag trains from a special recessed loading point accessed each side by a sunken single track that puts the wagons below the level of the discharge chutes. These trains then proceed to the major slag heap beyond Wulong Mine on the outskirts of Fuxin, but approach it via the line that runs below and avoids the big Wulong marshalling yard.

HEGANG (Heilongjiang Province)

The fleet at Hegang is noteworthy as it includes the first EL2s

Benxi's no. 1004, dating from 1972, has just left one of the marshalling yards. It is not equipped for dual control, now with the supplementary cooling device for the compressor. It does have side current collectors which is strange, given that there are no side-wire sections at Benxi itself. A possible explanation may be that it is so fitted to be able to work if needed also at Benxi's associated iron-ore mine at Waitoushan, where such sections are very likely to exist.

exported to China, a group of 16 given local running numbers starting from 1401. This happened in 1957 (see Zeitzeugnisse, Referenzen), though the works plates are dated 1956. The locomotives are plainer compared to later batches as they are not equipped for dual-control, nor do they have the cooling apparatus at the front end used in conjunction with increased cooling for the compressor for the traction motor blowers. A significant feature of these early EL2s is their short roof, with very little overhang, which marks them out from later batches and also serves to identity them despite the fact that several of them have been renumbered with higher numbers than 1416. Also characteristic is the method that has been used to strengthen the cab side-panels, where an X-shaped pressing has been made into the metal. They are fitted with side collectors - though in this early batch these are fitted in reverse compared to later examples, by which I mean that on the left-hand side of the locomotive they are placed over the front bogie, not the rear one. There were still three examples of this type at work at Hegang in the summer of 2002, two used as pilots in the main locomotive and rolling stock repair and maintenance works, and one still employed on regular duties at Lingbei North pit - hence the need for side collectors.

These first 16 EL2s appear to have been sufficient for Hegang's needs for a number of years - though there is evidence that pre-war Japanese-built 85-tonners were also active alongside them - as it was not until 1974 that newer EL2s were introduced. Thereafter, representatives of batches from 1980, 1981 and 1984 - the latter the last year in which EL2s were exported to China - were introduced to give a spread of manufacturing dates equalled only at Anshan.

PINGZHUANG (Inner Mongolia)

Pingzhuang has an extensive and complicated mine railway system centred round a large L-shaped open-cast pit. As far as electric industrial locomotives are concerned it uses EL2s exclusively, 37 of which are on the roster at present, from the three last (1980, 1981 and 1984) export batches. These have running numbers based on their works numbers, a 67xx series for the 1980 batch, and a 73xx series for the other two.

The pit was very active in the summer of 2002 and up to 12 or 13 EL2-hauled trains could be seen at work, or waiting to load, at any one time. One can gauge the level of activity from the frequent explosions which can be felt through the soles of one's feet - though they do not seem to deter the local population of ground squirrels nor prevent flocks of cows and goats being grazed. In summer the surroundings are not unpleasant up on the rim of the pit and in its vicinity where there is plenty of greenery and trees, and the ground is still fertile enough to support a number of small farms and their vegetable plots, while the woods provide mushroom collectors with good pickings.

QITAIHE (Heilongjiang Province)

Qitaihe has, if not the smallest mine railway system where LEW locomotives are to be found, the smallest total number of industrial electric locomotives and only four EL2s. All this railway's stock is maintained in top-class external condition. Despite the fact that all four come from the final 1984 batch exported to China, there is one aberrant example where a plate numbered 9211 of 1960 has for some mysterious reason found its way onto one side of #1004. This can be seen on close examination on the photograph provided of this locomotive. 9211 is not even an EL2 works plate, but comes in fact from the first EL1 to have gone to China. It would have been interesting to find out how this transfer was effected, or why, but unfortunately no explanation could be had.

Qitaihe is situated less conveniently than some of the other sites, particularly those within easy reach of Shenyang, as the train services to Jiamusi or Mudanjiang, the nearest large cities, are not particularly frequent. For this reason it has not been visited as often as other LEW sites.

References: Zeitzeugnisse, Parts I and II
Deutsche Eisenbahntechnik, May & August 1964.

100-ton ELECTRIC INDUSTRIAL LOCOMOTIVE EL2

Principal Technical Data

Type		EL 2/01	EL 2/05	EL 2/07	EL 2/17	EL 2/18	EL 2/19	EL 2/20	EL 2/22	EL 2/23
Service weight	t	100	100	100	100	100	100	100	100	100
Wheel Arrangement		Bo'Bo'	Bo'Bo'	Bo'Bo'	Bo'Bo'	Bo'Bo'	Bo'Bo'	Bo'Bo'	Bo'Bo'	
Axle Load	kN/Mp	245/25	245/25	245/25	245/25	245/25	245/25	245/25	245/25	100
Gauge	mm	1,435	1,524	1,435	1,435	1,435	1,435	1,435	1,435	
Length over Couplings	mm	13,700	13,820	13,700	13,700	13,545	13,700	13,700	13,700	13,545
Height above Top of Rail with lowered Pantograph	mm	4,050	4,660	4,050	4,050	4,660	4,050	4,050	4,050	4,050
Maximum Width	mm	3,100	3,200	3,100	3,100	3,200	3,100	3,100	3,100	3,200
Height of Coupling above Top of Rail	mm	1,020	1,055	1,020	1,020	880	1,020	1,020	1,020	
Diameter of Driving Wheels	mm	1,120	1,120	1,120	1,120	1,120	1,120	1,120	1,120	
Distance between Pivots	mm	6,250	6,150	6,250	6,250	6,150	6,250	6,250	6,250	
Bogie Wheelbase	mm	2,500	2,500	2,500	2,500	2,500	2,500	2,500	2,500	
Total Wheelbase	mm	8,800	8,700	8,800	8,800	8,700	8,800	8,800	8,800	
Minimum Curve at v = 5 kph	m	50	50	50	80	50	80	80	80	50
Coefficient of Weight Transfer from Axle at 30 Mp of Tractive Effort	%	0.9	0.9	0.9	0.9	0.91	0.9	0.9	0.9	
Pneumatic Brake System		Knorr	Matrossov	Knorr	Knorr	Knorr	Knorr	Knorr	Knorr	
Compressor Output	m3/h	120	300	300	120	450	300	126	300	
Normal Voltage of Contact Line	V	1,200/2,400	1,500	1,500	1,200/2,400	1,500	1,500	1,200/2,400	1,500	1,500
One-hour Rating of Traction Motors at 25C	kW	4x350	4x350	4x350	4x345	4x350	4x350	4x350	4x350	1,400 (4x350)
Speed at one-hour Rating	km/h	28	30	30	28.8	30	31	28.8	30	
Tractive Effort at one-hour Rating	kN/Mp	170/17.0	165/16.5	165/16.5	170/17.0	162/16.2	165/16.5	167/16.7	162/16.2	16,700/16.7
Continuous Rating of Traction Motors at 25C	kW	4x290	4x290	4x290	4x290	4x290	4x290	4x290	4x290	1,160 (4x290)
Tractive Effort at continuous Rating	kN/Mp	132/13.2	126/12.6	126/12.6	133/13.3	123/12.3	125/12.5	130/13.0	123/12.3	12,900/12.9
Speed at continuous Rating	km/h	31.0	32.8	32.8	-	33	-	30.6	33	
Maximum permitted Speed	km/h	65	65	65	65	70	65	65	65	70
Maximum Tractive Effort on Starting at mu = 0.33	kN/Mp	294/30	294/30	294/30	294/30	294/30	294/30	294/30	294/30	30
Control Voltage	V	48	48	48	48	48	48	48	48	
Method of Control		Contactor Control	Contactor Control	Contactor Control	Contactor Control	Contactor Control	Contactor Control	Contactor Control	Contactor Control	
Number of Traction Notches		34	34	34	34	34	34	34	34	
Number of Brake Notches		22	22	22	22	22	22	22	22	
Electric Brake System		Rheostatic Brake	Rheostatic Brake	Rheostatic Brake	Rheostatic Brake	Rheostatic Brake	Rheostatic Brake	Rheostatic Brake	Rheostatic Brake	
Battery Capacity	Ah	150	150	150	100	100	100	100	100	
Gear Ratio		1:5.58	1:5.58	1:5.58	1:5.58	1:5.58	1:5.58	1:5.58	1:5.58	
Multiple Control		2 Locomotives	2 Locomotives	2 Locomotives	2 Locomotives	-	2 Locomotives	2 Locomotives	2 Locomotives	
Output of Control Current Generator	kW	3	4.5	3	3	4.5	3	2x1.5	2x1.5	

Note: The EL2/23 variant was built for use in China. The technical details are taken from the specifications plates these locomotives carry.

Note: EL2s frequently still carry a specifications plate, in Chinese, in addition to the LEW works plate. It is thought that this plate was prepared in Hennigsdorf to Chinese designs, and fitted there, in much the same way as some running numbers were already applied before the engines left the DDR - the example of #7405 mentioned later is a case in point. They omit some of the details available from the data tables in Zeitzeugnisse, but add two further categories, the minimum negotiable radius and the width of the engine.

Well, almost none!